The Graphic Legacy of
PAUL KLEE

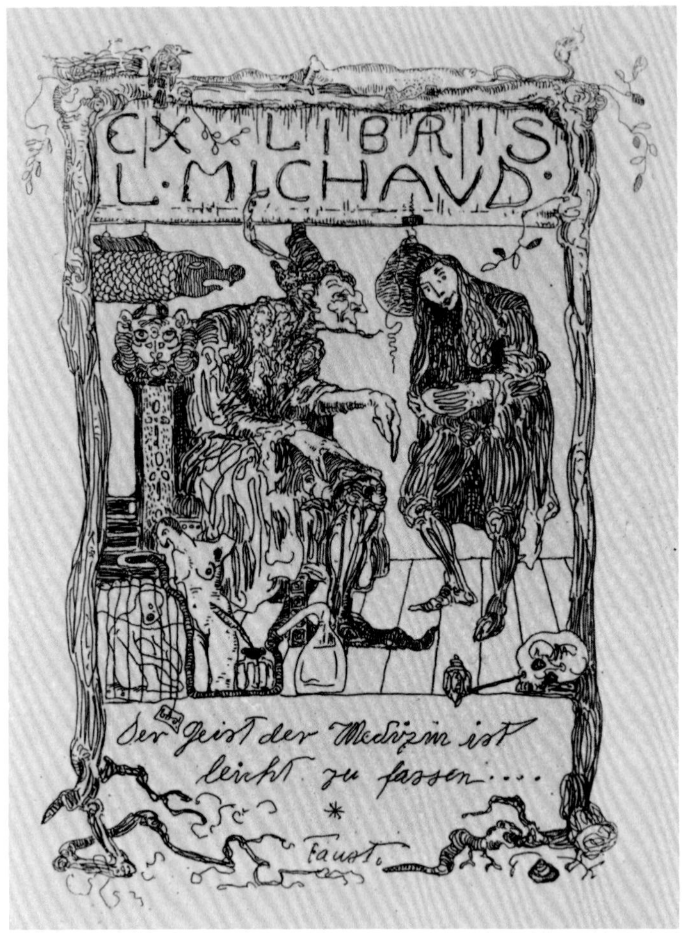

Ex Libris L. Michaud, *1901. Etching, 158 × 116 mm.*
Collection of Felix Klee, Bern, Switzerland. (K 2)

The Graphic Legacy of PAUL KLEE

AN EXHIBITION OF KLEE'S PRINTS

October 23—December 28, 1983—Bard College

Published by the
Edith C. Blum Art Institute
Milton and Sally Avery Center for the Arts
The Bard College Center

Annandale-on-Hudson, New York

Published by Bard College
Edith C. Blum Art Institute
Annandale-on-Hudson, NY

Front Cover: Paul Klee, *Hoffmannesque Scene,* 1921. Colored lithograph, 316 × 230 mm. (plate)
Back Cover: *A Genius Serves A Little Breakfast* 1920 Lithograph, hand colored, 255 × 175 mm.
End papers: Detail of *Small World,* 1914.
Etching on zinc, 145 × 96 mm. (plate).

Catalog Design: John O'Mara
Printed at: Morgan Press, Inc.
Dobbs Ferry, NY

Library of Congress Catalogue
Card Number 83-72731
ISBN 0-941276-03-1
Edition limited to 2,000 copies

This exhibition is funded with the aid of generous grants from Sandoz, Inc., the National Endowment for the Arts, and the New York State Council on the Arts with contributions from Credit Suisse, Swiss Reinsurance, and the Renker-Moss Foundation.

Preface

This exhibit reflects the ambition and the achievement of the Edith C. Blum Art Institute and the Milton and Sally Avery Center for the Arts. Only the most optimistic of the founders of these two institutions would have believed that in fewer than three years since the founding of these entities, a comprehensive and critically significant exhibition of the work of a major twentieth century artist would originate at Bard. The credit for this progress goes to our staff and benefactors, whose idealism and persistence (not to mention skill) made this exhibition of the graphic work of Paul Klee possible.

Paul Klee's work has an authentic intimacy, born out of Klee's capacity to invent continuously with line and structure; to transmit the logic of his imagination in the language of art; and to grace his art with an integral humor. Klee was neither follower nor leader; his originality was neither labored nor the consequence of a self-conscious search for a signature and a style. Yet few artists in the twentieth century have become so popular. Klee's fantasy and intricate use of color and shape have touched the hearts and challenged the intellects of more than four generations.

Paul Klee's command of musical language, his attachment to the Viennese classical repertoire and his knowledge of the legato and filigree ornamental qualities of the violin are visible in his work and in his mode of composition and invention. This exhibition highlights some of the most musical of Klee's work.

It is fitting that Bard not only mount an exhibit but also seek to illuminate the musical dimensions in the graphic work of Paul Klee. This college, the Blum Institute (where many concerts are held throughout the year) and the Avery Center (which includes drama and dance)—particularly the Milton Avery Graduate School of the Arts—are dedicated to the arts, not merely as discrete disciplines, but as languages of expression and invention whose power and source are closely interrelated. This exhibition reflects this credo.

I would like to thank all those who have produced this exhibition and catalogue. Their quality is a reminder that smallness of scale can be a virtue; that smallness can enhance excellence and succeed in a world dominated by massive size and extensive concentrations of resources. Bard is honored to underscore this faith through Paul Klee's work. The beauty and magic of his vision and achievement are an inspiration. Size itself may not stand as a barrier to our highest hopes.

Leon Botstein,
President of Bard College

Detail of Virgin in a Tree, *1903.*
Etching on zinc, 236 × 298 mm. (plate).

Acknowledgements

Nowhere are Klee's metaphysical journeys more poignantly recorded than in his prints. Through extreme abbreviation, the magic of a dot, expanding to become a line, spreading to form a plane, and made to suggest a space are all condensed within this graphic medium. They provide a summary of his entire career and form, at the same time, a discrete body of work.

Paul Klee was able to sustain, throughout his life, the creative crescendo of his youth. His output was prodigious, his energy unabated, propelled by seemingly contradictory motivations: a keen grasp of reality and an anguished grappling with the uncertainties of existence. Klee sought to reconcile this dilemma through the creation of art, penetrating distant psychological dimensions, domains that were too bright, too deep, too intense to be tolerated within the space of ordinary existence.

Despite his prolific output, Klee produced, in his life, only 109 prints. It is one aspect of his career that has not yet been thoroughly examined. The Edith C. Blum Art Institute is privileged to present the most comprehensive exhibition of Klee's prints that has ever been organized. This privilege has evolved out of the combined efforts of innumerable individuals, each contributing in some vital and unique way to fulfilling this ambitious task. It is the beauty of the exhibition and the appreciation of the visitors that will serve as the enduring form of gratitude. To them I would like to add a few phrases so that the specific roles of each will be recognized by all.

Carl Djerassi, the distinguished organic chemist, whose fascination with the fragmentary and dynamic world observed through a microscope has found its artistic counterpart in the prints of Paul Klee. Dr. Djerassi has not only allowed the Edith C. Blum Art Institute to borrow his entire collection, but he has been instrumental in the fund raising for this exhibition. In addition, the poem that he wrote serves as a spirited introduction to the exhibition catalogue.

Jean de Castella de Delley and Hart Perry, active supporters of Bard College and effective liasons between the Art Institute and the Swiss lenders and Swiss contributors. Barbara Haskell, who has been a loyal supporter of the exhibition program at Bard College, provided decisive and much appreciated advice regarding this exhibition. Their participation was essential to the success of this project.

Jim Jordan, exhibition curator, who has guided the course of this exhibition and its catalogue with diligence and patience, assuring its contribution to the scholarship regarding this great artist. Jeff Weiss served as research assistant and Melanie Feit as translator.

Felix Klee, editor of Paul Klee's diaries, Jürgen Glaesemer, Curator of the Klee Foundation, Kunstmuseum Bern, and Christian Geelhaar, Director, Kunstammlung Basel, the most eminently respected Klee scholars in Europe, who shared the wealth of their knowledge with English speaking audiences by contributing essays to this catalogue.

James Wood and Cathryn Lee of the Art Institute of Chicago who exhibited a truly impressive commitment to our exhibition. Their cooperation and support has demonstrated the fact that the bureaucratic structure of a major art museum need not destroy its ability to preserve a sympathetic and flexible stance.

President Leon Botstein and Executive Vice President Dimitri Papadimitriou who, although they have always been active supporters of the Edith C. Blum Art Institute, have made a very special effort to assure the success of this exhibition.

Charles Gillieron, Consul of Cultural Affairs, Ambassador Ernst Andres, Consul General of Switzerland, and Gilbert Schlaefli, Swiss Consul, who were gracious advisers in this project.

Christina Flocken, Donise English, Karla Paschkis, Mike Prudhom, Judy Samoff, Brian Harris, Charles Schuman, and Tina Iraca, whose dedication to this exhibition made possible the complicated task of arranging the loans of work from the United States and Europe, of applying for grants, and of publicizing the event to a broad public. Heinz and Leila Bertelsman, Robert Kelly, Andrew Kagan, Dorothy Miller, Amie Zeitler, Roman Totenberg, and Hugo Munsterberg have also participated in this project, each contributing his or her special talent.

John O'Mara and Doug Morgan were tireless in their efforts to assure that the quality of the catalogue reflected the nature of the exhibition it commemorated.

Sandoz, Inc., The National Endowment for the Arts, and The New York State Council for the Arts who made substantial contributions to this project. Their commitment made it possible to realize a plan that seemed, at times, to exceed the realm of possibility. Gratitude is also extended to the Swiss Reinsurance Company, Credit Suisse and the Renker Moss Foundation, Inc. for their generous contributions.

The lenders, all of whom came to appreciate the goals of this project and to share in fulfilling its potential. Through their cooperation, the most extensive examination of Paul Klee's accomplishments as graphic artist was achieved.

Linda Weintraub
Institute Director

Lenders to the Exhibition

Alice Adam Gallery
Art Institute of Chicago
Hans Bolliger
Busch-Reisinger Museum, Harvard
Dartmouth College Library
Professor Carl Djerassi
Galerie Rosengart
James Gilvarry
Robert Gore Rifkind Center for German Expressionist Studies, The Robert Gore Rifkind Foundation, The Los Angeles County Museum of Art.
Felix Klee
Eberhard Kornfeld
Kunstammlung Basel
Kunstmuseum Bern
Maureen M. Morgan
Museum of Modern Art
Philadelphia Museum of Art Library
Stadtische Galerie im Lenbachhaus

Contents

Preface 5

Acknowledgements 7

Paul Klee at Bard
by Carl Djerassi 10

My Thoughts About the Prints of Paul Klee
by Felix Klee 13

Paul Klee: Chronology 22

Introduction to the Exhibition
by Jim Jordan 27

Paul Klee's Small Graphic World: 1912-1932
by Christian Geelhaar 49

Paul Klee's Prints
by Jürgen Glaesemer 69

Klee's Prints and Oil Transfer Works: Some Further Reflections
by Jim Jordan 87

Exhibition Check List 114

Paul Klee at Bard

By Carl Djerassi

I wonder how Paul Klee would have felt—He, the arch-European,
He, the most intellectual of intellectual painters—
That in America, which he had never visited
(Tunisia was far and strange enough),
In the small but exquisite museum of
A small but exquisite college, named Bard
(Itself an ambiguous and provocative name)
There would be an exhibition of his work.
Not all of it. Only a small portion.
Say 1% of it, but an important 1%.

Paul Klee! We are speaking of your graphic work.
Have even you seen so much of it
In one place, at one time?
Especially, years after the last work was completed.
When nothing could be added; your mind not changed any more.
Errors not correctable.
To be seen, to be studied, to be savored.

The last word is the most important. Savored.

It is not easy to savor huge canvasses, enormous strokes of paint,
Big visual impacts, inherent shock values—
Such art is not unimportant, not insignificant. Far from it.
It can be seen, studied and appreciated.
But savored? Hardly.

"Die Verse zu diesen Reimen waren zu sehr erdacht,
. . . und zu wenig getraumt
und entstanden doch in einer hellen Stunde. . ."
Paul Klee (1901)

Is this why I, who studies miniscule particles of matter, molecules—
Professor of Chemistry, not Art—
Have always been enamored of your work?
Am captivated by the huge complexity, yet small dimensions of your space,
By you, the painter *par excellence* of the *petit format?*
I savor it.

Why do we focus on your graphic work,
So small a portion of your total *oeuvre?*
Because it manifests the possibility
Of achieving the impossible:
To focus in one frame, one room, one time,
On virtually all you conceived and accomplished in one medium.
Drawings? Impossible. Too many. Too diverse.
Watercolors? Impossible. Too many. Too diverse.
Oils? Impossible. Fewer but not affordable (to me).
Puppets? Very few. None collectable.
Graphics? The etchings, lithographs, woodcuts? Perhaps.
This small museum of this small college will provide the answer.

Stanford University

Photograph of Paul Klee from a Sturm Postcard, 1918.
Photographer: Paula Stokmar.

My Thoughts About the Prints of Paul Klee

By Felix Klee

I have often had the opportunity to compare the printed work of Paul Klee with its different states and preliminary studies in exhibitions. With what thoroughness did my father conceive and form the works during certain periods. In this essay I wish to pursue closely the entire chronological development: The catalogue of Klee's graphic work by Mr. E. W. Kornfeld (hereafter indicated as Kfd.) serves as a basis for my reflections. This record appeared 20 years ago and consists of two parts: first the number 1-109 and then numbers A-110 through A-150. These special works constitute, to be sure, only a small part of the 10,000 or so works of art in Klee's oeuvre. But what importance they have in conjunction with the more than 5000 drawings!

The earliest work is a "beercard" of September 24, 1898 (Kfd A-110) which Klee conceived with his already pronounced sarcastic humour. He wrote in his diary entry no. 63 about this time: "After having barely passed my final examination, I began to paint in Munich."

In Klee's diary entry no. 71 we find the first reference to work with prints: "Burghausen-Salzburg 1899: Before leaving I accepted the invitation of Ziegler the etcher to visit him in his little castle nearby. When I rang the bell I was deafened by the barks of a monstrous dog. I liked it better upstairs. Ziegler showed me his material for the book he was planning on etching. There was something attractive about his laboratory." I believe that Klee received a lot of encouragement for later etchings from this visit. In a letter of July 17, 1899, we learn even more about this meeting: "I have met here a very well known etching artist called Ziegler, especially well-known as a technician. He has seen my sketch book and has invited me to visit him. He wants to tell me the essentials about etching, aquatint, etc., so that I will probably be ready to do all kinds of experiments in Bern. Next winter I will test all the existing techniques, etching, lithography, as a direct black and white process. I know how to draw and nobody on this earth can possibly teach me the arts mentioned above.—I have already acquired in my drawings a very special linear technique. With it I have always instinctively thought about etching, so that this technique almost naturally leads to etching, as Herr Ziegler suggested. I will therefore first go to Ziegler's, to see his plates and instruments and to pick up the promised pamphlet."

The first result was 1901,1 (Kfd 1), created in May of that year: It is a "fantastic fish," which is preserved only in two impressions. Of all the numerous fish generated by Klee's imagination, this specimen is indeed the strangest, like a fossil from prehistoric times.

Il. 2 **B**ut let us move on: During the summer of 1901 Klee made an *Ex Libris* (Kfd 2) for his friend Michaud, and inscribed on it for the young medical student words of Goethe: "The spirit of medicine is easy to capture—FAUST."

1903, Estate (Kfd 3) *Woman and Beast,* first version. About this, Klee wrote on July 12, 1903: "The beast is the beast in the human being, in man. He annoys a woman first by improperly smelling her.—Clarification of the human."

Il. 15 1903,2 (Kfd 4) *Virgin in a Tree (Dreaming).* Concerning this print, Klee noted in his diary 1903, no. 514: "Technically more mature, thanks to the use of lines of varying heaviness. First I scratched and etched the contours of the tree. Then, the modeling of the tree and the contours of the body, then the modeling of the bodies and the pair of birds. The poetic content resembles, at bottom, that of *Woman and Beast.* The beasts (the birds) are natural and paired. The lady wants to be something special through virginity, but doesn't cut an attractive figure. Critique of bourgeois society."

Three versions exist of the etching *Comedian,* 1903,3; 1904,10 and 1904,14. In the second version (Kfd 9) Klee depicts himself behind the mask. He himself is serious, while the mask leers slightly. Intention of his style: "Sarcasm, parody, and to make seriousness appear ridiculous."

Let us now consider 1903,4 (Kfd 5) *Woman, Sowing Weeds.* About this Klee wrote on July 12, 1903: "Yesterday a second, much smaller and less pretentious plate was printed. It shows a small feminine nude . . . bold, droll, twisting, and turning. With her hands she casts grains into the air . . ."

Il. 19 **C**ontinuing with 1903, 5 (Kfd 7) *Two Men Meet, Each Supposing the Other to be of Higher Rank,* "Invention" no. 6. Klee wrote the following in his diary, 1903, no. 519: "On September 14th, all is empty around me, cold and wasted, nasty and cursed. Then I worked furiously, much more than the lone result could show. I looked for consolation in it for my social position. The first time, impatience made me etch the preliminary sketch too soon; then I went at the composition again and improved it considerably. With the etching, too, I had better luck than the first time." A friend of our family drew my attention to the suggestion that the two men had a strong resemblance to Kaiser Wilhelm II and Emperor Franz-Josef of Austria. I wouldn't contradict him. Could it be that Klee also thought of this? It could easily be expected of him.

1904, Estate, July (Kfd 11) *Pessimistic Symbolism of the Mountain,* "Invention" 11. We can read in Klee's letter of July 16, 1904: "The work is quite a bad joke, wherein

Virgin in the Tree, *1903. Etching on zinc, 236 × 298 mm. (plate). Collection of Professor Carl Djerassi, Stanford University. (K 4b)*

the mountain is compared to a monumental figure, whose head and one arm are tangled up in a strange cloth."

Il. 26 1905, 38 (Kfd 16) *The Hero with the Wing.* This etching received a good explanation in the inscription: "Being born with one wing, he therefore has the idea that he was predestined to fly, which kills him."

Il. 29 1905, 36 (Kfd 17) *Aged Phoenix,* "Invention" no. 9. In a letter of February 19, 1905 Klee wrote: "It is difficult for me to talk about my most recent etching. I have (created) an allegory of inadequacy as a resurrecting phoenix, pictorially very original. One should imagine for example, that there had just been a cycle, the inadequacy had been burnt, and now it rises rejuvenated from its own ashes. This is my faith."

Il. 31 1905, 37 (Kfd 18) *The Menacing Head.* I have always been fascinated with this rodent with stag-like antlers, over the head bearing features of a self-portrait. Concerning this, Klee wrote in his diary entries 602 and 603: ". . . I am almost inclined to believe that this will be the last print in the strict style and that something entirely new will follow. I turn my eye towards Spain where Goyas grow.—The end is gloomy enough. Some destructive thought or other, a sharply negative little demon above a hopelessly resigned face."

After the "Inventions" of the year 1903-1905 we recognize in 1907 a complete stylistic change in Klee's prints; for example 1907, 24 (Kfd 20) *Two Nudes at the Sea* and 1907, Estate, (Kfd 21) *The Drinker.* About them Klee wrote in his diary no. 801: "I try to carry over what I learned from my charcoal drawings from nature into free composition."

Il. 48 The etching 1910, 22 (Kfd 23) *New Avenue* represents in two versions the flat, slightly dreary surroundings of Munich. In other etchings, like 1910, 106 (Kfd 25) *Garden,* Klee began to work on celluloid. 1910, 114 (Kfd 29) *Speed-boat,* a dry-point, was executed in a painterly manner. 1911, Estate, (Kfd 36) *Concert Hall* represents a melancholic remembrance of the magnificent Odeon-hall in Munich. As a child I often heard wonderful concerts there with my parents in the era of Bruno Walter. Unfortunately, the house was totally destroyed during the last war and has not been reconstructed.

Il. 47 1911, 25 (Kfd 37) *Railway Station.* This etching, a dry-point on celluloid, also reminds me of my youth, when for hours I used to watch the railway yard with enthusiasm from the Hacker bridge in Munich. Those many locomotives probably produced more pollution in those days than today's electric power.

1912, Estate (Kfd 41) *Landscape near Milbertshofen.* This suburb of Munich, which for a long time has been part of the city, was once a small Bavarian village to which I often accompanied my father. He drew and painted there in the rustic, idyllic surroundings; I helped him carry things and during breaks he would play with me.

The year 1912 was very important for Klee's printed work. We find at that time a large number of "lithographic essays" on transfer paper, which Kornfeld presents under the category "A." As Klee created just one copy of each and did not print

Comedian, *1903. Etching on zinc, 118 × 161 mm. (ohne Facette).*
Collection of Oeffentliche Kunstsammlung Basel, Kupferstichkabinett. (K 6)

them, I therefore choose to classify them as "drawings." What imagination flourishes here in numerous rich, occasionally religious themes, such as 1912, 138 (Kfd A115) *The Higher Spirit Mourning for the Lower One;* 1912, 139 (Kfd A 116) *Martyrdom;* 1912, 140 (Kfd A 117) *Doubt Upwards;* 1912, 141 (Kfd A 118) *The Child and His Star;* and 1912, 143 (Kfd A 120) *Flight to the Stars.* This series was extended into Klee's prints
Il. 55 with the following: 1912, 117 (Kfd 46) *St. George;* 1912, 118 (Kfd 47) *Street Urchins;* and 1912, 119 (Kfd 48) *Tragedy on Stilts.*

1912, 3 (Kfd 43) *Nude.* This female nude reappears in a nearly identical drawing from Klee's last year in Bern.

In 1913 the influence of a journey to Paris can be perceived: 1913, 29 (Kfd 55) *Pomp in Miniature.* Here we find for the first time cubistic and abstract forms. The word 'miniature' refers only to the format of the etching: 7.5 × 5.9 cm.

Il. 57 1913, 155 (Kfd 56) *Garden of Passion,* a now famous print. In the encoded abstract forms we discover certain parallels with the *Garden of Earthly Delights* by Hieronymous Bosch.

We see further abstract forms in the following prints, 1913, 178 (Kfd 57) *Plants at*
Il. 65 *Night in the Rain;* 1913, 179 (Kfd 58) *Abstraction I;* 1913, 182 (Kfd 59) *Abstraction II* and in further examples from the years 1914 and 1915.

World War I was deeply incorporated into some of the works: 1916, 53 (Kfd 67) *Suicide on the Bridge* and, above all, in the hand-watercolored lithograph 1916, 55
Il. 67 (Kfd 68) *Destruction and Hope* or "Ruins and Hopes." The three heavenly signs, the sun, moon, and stars constitute a positive contrast to the cruel present.

The war is over. In the years 1915 and 1920 some lithographs followed with various themes. From 1921 on Klee could better supervise his graphic production in the printing workshop at the Weimar Bauhaus. Color was also added: 1920, 91 (Kfd 79) *A*
Il. 106/107 *Genius Serving a Small Breakfast.* This work also received a subtitle: *Angel Bringing the Desired.* How often in times of crisis one needs a genius, who helps to surmount despair. Klee water-colored the impression with brilliant, mostly red colors.

The following lithographs were printed in color at the Bauhaus: 1921, 22 (Kfd 81)
Il. 91/93 *The Saint of Inner Light* and 1921, 123 (Kfd 82) *Hoffmannesque Scene.*

In 1923 the Bauhaus celebrated its five year anniversary, with important exhibitions. The form masters designed post cards, some printed in color, some watercolored by hand. Such was true for Klee: 1922, Estate (Kfd 87) *Lantern Festival*
Il. 111 *Bauhaus;* 1923, 47 (Kfd 88) *The Sublime Aspect;* and, in contrast to the academic atmosphere, 1923, (Kfd 89) *The Cheerful Aspect.*

1923, 91 (Kfd 94) The Lover. Here, as in a kind of love obsession, the girl is represented wedged in the head of the adolescent. How often this happens in life!

Il. 113 **A** splendid colorful lithograph is 1923, 138 (Kfd 95) *The Tightrope Walker.* His dangerous profession is firmly anchored by a white cross on a red field, a good omen of the artist returning safely to earth. Two works of the same subject should not be omitted from mention: 1923, 215 a preliminary drawing; and 1923, 121 a watercolor.

Two Men Meet, Each Supposing the Other of Higher Rank, *1903.*
Etching on zinc, 118 × 225 mm. (plate).
Collection of Professor Carl Djerassi, Stanford University. (K 7 IIa)

At a visit to the opera "Cosi fan tutte" by Mozart, in the Weimar National Theater,
Klee heard and admired the highly skilled singer and actress Priska Aich in the role of
"Fiordiligi." This performance was enough encouragement for Klee to execute the
Il. 97 lithograph 1925, W5 (225) (Kfd 99) *The Singer of the Comic Opera.* It is black and
white, and in some versions is sprayed in red watercolor. Klee was so excited about
this theme, that he created two other watercolors: 1923, 39 and 1923, 118 with the
title: *The Singer L. as Fiordiligi,* and finally an oil painting as well, 1927, 10, with the
same title.

Il. 121 The etching 1929, S9 (99) (Kfd 104) *Old Man Reckoning* was intended for an edition
of 130 copies for the members of the "Swiss Graphic Society." In those days the print
was much disliked and some temperamental recipients even destroyed the work. For
this etching there exists a beautiful preliminary drawing, which is almost identical
with the print. Indeed, the similarity of the drawing 1929, 0 10 (60) arouses my admiration. The old man is anxious and fears that his possessions might diminish, and thus
he has to count carefully. The expression of the face almost suggests greed with its
penetrating and cold gaze.

Unfortunately, I have to leave out some equally beautiful works. However, I still
Il. 123/122 wish to include the special etching 1931, R 17 (157) *L'homme approximatif (Eye and
Ear)* (Kfd 107). There is a year separating both the preliminary drawing 1929, 3 H 6
(306) *Eye and Ear*, and the painting 1930, AE 10 (270) *The Listener.* The gaze of the
listener, with the single eye of the painter, is composed quite similarly in all three versions. Klee himself was a violinist, a practicing musician. Thus the ear, concerned
with playing an instrument, but above all, listening to and enjoying enchanting music
or a fabulous language.

These reflections of mine are intended to guide the viewer a little, as over a bridge, to the "special way" of my father Paul Klee.

Felix Klee
(Bern, July 1983)

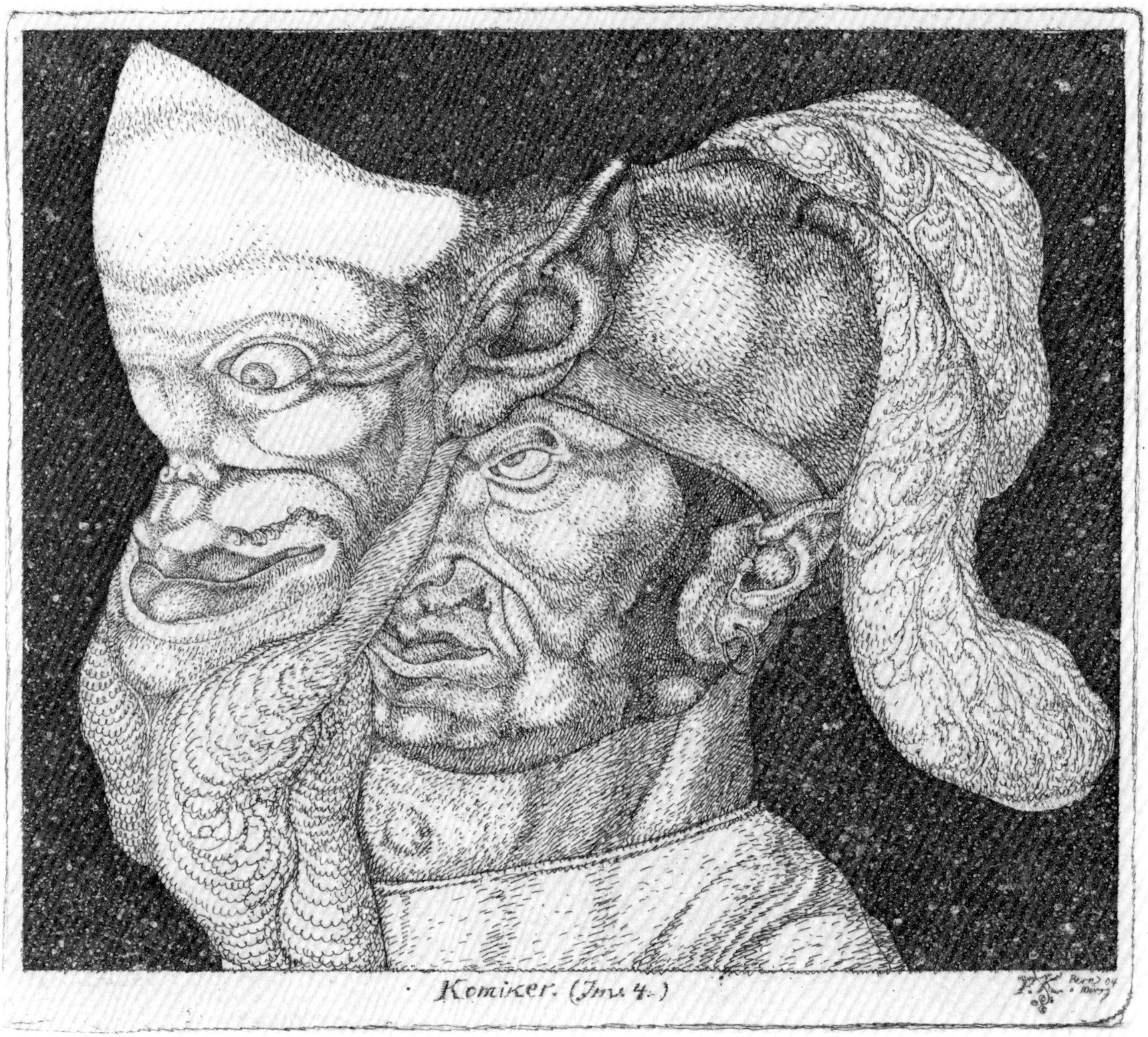

The Comedian, *1904. Etching on zinc, 153 × 168 mm. (plate).*
Collection of Professor Carl Djerassi, Stanford University. (K 10 IIb)

Paul Klee: Chronology

1879
18 December: Born in Münchenbuchsee near Bern, Switzerland where the Klees will settle in 1880. Both parents are musicians and raise their son with a deep love for classical music.

1883
First childhood drawings.

1886-97
Education in Bern.
Fills schoolbook margins with caricatures.
From age 7 studies violin.
From age 13 draws Swiss countryside.

1898-1900
Begins to keep a diary.
Graduates from Literarschule, Bern.

Moves to Munich to study art. Takes anatomy drawing at the private school of Heinrich Knirr, and at the Academy under Franz Stuck. Introduced by his friend Walter Ziegler to etching and engraving techniques.

Meets future wife, Lily Stumpf, at a musical soirée.

Between 1898-1906, will attempt to publish caricatural drawings in German and Swiss satirical magazines.

1901
March: Leaves Academy, dissatisfied with Stuck's instruction.

May: First print, a zinc plate etching *Fantastic Fish.*

Struggle between poetry, painting and music as "ideal" profession.

October: Embarks on a six month journey to Italy with artist and boyhood friend Herman Haller. Stops in Genoa, Pisa, Rome, Naples, Florence. Especially admires Botticelli and Leonardo as colorists, antique sculpture, an exhibition of Rodin drawings, Naples aquarium and, as a lesson in composition and spatial organization of design elements, antique and medieval architecture.

1902
May: Returns from Italy. In his diary, he is perplexed by the towering greatness of the Classical tradition and its waning relevance as a source for contemporary art.

Through 1906, lives with parents in Bern.

1903
July: Begins series of 10 allegorical-satirical etchings which, in a musical frame of mind, he refers to as "Inventions," later as "Opus 1."

1904
Work on "Invention" series continues.

October: Visits Munich Museum print room. Admires works by Goya, Blake and Beardsley.

1905
"Invention" series concluded.

Continues to explore grotesque distortions of the human body in a summary drawing manner perhaps inspired by children's art.

1906
June: First trip to Paris with painters Louis Moilliet and Hans Bloesch. Admires painters who explore a limited color range and rich tonalities: Leonardo, Rembrandt, Velazquez, Carriere, Puvis de Chavannes, Whistler, Goya.

Summer: Experiments with drawings scratched on a blackened pane of glass.

Autumn: Begins painting on glass,cultivating a more fluid brushwork largely in black and white.

September: Marries Lily Stumpf and moves to Munich. She supports them by teaching music.

The 10 "Inventions" appear in Munich Secession, framed together as a series. The "Inventions" are rejected, however, for publication by the satirical journal *Simplicissimus.*

1907
Introduced by his friend Ernst Sonderegger to drawings and illustrations by Ensor and Daumier. Also admires graphic works of Toulouse-Lautrec.

November: Birth of son Felix.

1908
Through 1911, produces "Impressionist" pen and ink-wash pictures which utilize his own drawing technique of "light forms" to examine effects of light in nature.

1910
Meets Alfred Kubin.

August-January, 1911: First one-man exhibition in Switzerland of 56 works from 1907-10.

Intense work on prints during this year.

1911
Meets Wassily Kandinsky, Franz Marc and August Macke, members of the newly-formed expressionist group *Der Blaue Reiter.*

February: Begins to catalogue his past and present work. Included are 18 childhood drawings, and only two done while studying with Knirr and Stuck.

Transcribes previous diaries, adding childhood memories.

March: Begins illustrations for Voltaire's *Candide* in a terse, attenuated manner of figuration.

Summer: Founding member of the artists' group *Sema* or "sign." Contributes a lithograph to their collector's portfolio of graphic works.

November-January, 1913: Reviews exhibitions and other cultural events in Munich for the Swiss monthly *Die Alpen.*

December: First exposure to the cubist works of Robert Delaunay at the premier exhibition of *Blaue Der Reiter* in Munich.

1912
March: Participates with 17 drawings in a *Blaue Reiter* exhibition of watercolors and graphics, which included works of Picasso and Braque.

April: Second trip to Paris, where he visits the studios of Delaunay and Henri Le Fauconnier, and familiarizes himself further with the cubism of Picasso and Braque.

Summer: Works included in an exhibition of the Swiss *Moderner Bund* in Zurich.

Winter: Sees an exhibition of Italian Futurism at the Thannhauser Gallery in Munich.

During 1912, executes four tentative woodblock prints, 10 lithographs, and a number of drawings on lithographic transfer paper which may have been intended for printing. As expressed in a letter to Alfred Kubin, considers printmaking less for its distinctive formal possibilities than as a means for exposing work to a larger public.

1913
January: His translation of Delaunay's essay "On Light" appears in the periodical *Der Sturm.*

Invited by Marc to join Kandinsky, Kubin, Oskar Kokoschka and Erich Heckel as a contributor to an illustrated *Blaue Reiter* edition of the Bible, a project which remained unrealized.

September-December: Works included in the First German Autumn Salon, a large survey of the international avant-garde at Herwarth Walden's Sturm Gallery in Berlin.

Drawings and etchings evolve under the crucial influence of Cubism; especially important is the structured pictorial space of a cubistic linear scaffolding.

1914
April: Journey to Tunisia with Louis Moilliet and August Macke. Under the influence of Delaunay's Orphic Cubism, works done in Tunisia mark first efforts as a confident and inspired colorist.

August: Outbreak of World War I. Stays on in Munich. Kandinsky emigrates to Switzerland. Marc and Macke called up; Macke is killed in battle, 16 August.

Commissioned by periodical *Zeit-Echo* for a picture to accompany a poem by Theodor Daubler, Klee executes his lithograph *Battlefield.*

1915
First tentative efforts at sculpture in plaster. Signs a contract with art dealer Hans Goltz.

1916
March: Called up by the German army. Serves first in infantry at Landshut, then at Flying School in Schleissheim where he paints aircraft and accompanies convoys. His attitude toward the war is one of cool, occasionally ironic detachment.

October: Colors with stencils the lithograph *Destruction and Hope.*

1917
Transferred to Gersthofen.

Exhibitions at the Sturm Gallery. Sells successfully through Walden and Goltz.

1918
September: Initial draft of "Creative Credo," his first formal philosophical statement on art and creativity.

November: Commissioned to illustrate *Potsdamer Platz oder die Nachte des Neuen Messias,* a novel by the German expressionist writer Curt Corrinth.

By the end of 1918, Klee has produced 69 of his lifetime output of 109 prints.

1919
February: Demobilized. Works again in Munich.

July: Potential job offer from Stuttgart Academy of Art falls through.

Journal *Kestnerbuch* publishes a 1919 lithograph. *Münchner Blätter für Dichtung und Graphik* publishes 6 1919 lithographs, including *Self-Portrait— Meditation* and *Number-Tree Landscape.*

1920
362 works in Retrospective at the Goltz Gallery.

October: Receives and accepts an offer from Walter Gropius to become a *Formmeister* at the newly estaliblished Bauhaus in Weimar. There he will develop a science of picturemaking in a series of lectures for classes on painting.

"Creative Credo" published in a collection of artist's writings edited by Kasimir Edschmid.

Monographs on Klee by Hans von Wedderkop and Leopold Zahn are published.

Candide with 26 illustrations published by Kurt Wolff.

Potsdamer Platz with 10 illustrations published by Georg Muller.

1921
Monograph on Klee by Wilhelm Hausenstein published.
October: Settles in Weimar. Two color-lithographs of 1921, *The Saint of Inner Light* and *Hoffmannesque Scene,* included in Bauhaus portfolio *New European Graphics. Masters of the National Bauhaus in Weimar.*

While at the Bauhaus in Weimar, produces 20 lithographs. Certain of these prints will appear with works by other contemporary German artists in collector's portfolios published outside of the Bauhaus, such as *Art of Today* in Munich, 1923.

1922
Hand-colored lithograph executed as a postcard for Bauhaus midsummer Lantern Festival. Kandinsky joins Bauhaus teaching staff.

1923
Essay "Ways of Nature Study" published by the Bauhaus.

Executes two color-lithograph postcards, of a series of 20 designed by Bauhaus faculty and students, for the Bauhaus Exhibition.

1923 color-lithograph *Man in Love* included in the *Master Portfolio of the National Bauhaus.*

1924
January: Delivers lecture, "On Modern Art," to

the Jena Artist's Association.

With Kandinsky, Lyonel Feininger and Alexei von Jawlensky forms the *Blaue Vier,* an association designed to further sales in the United States

First exhibition in the United States, sponsored by the *Societe Anonyme,* New York.

Klee Sociéty organized by Otto Ralfs and other collectors who agree to pay an annual subscription in return for original prints. *Female Singer of Comic Opera,* 1925, *Heights,* 1928 and *Juggler in April, 1928,* were created for this purpose.

December: The Bauhaus is closed by newly elected, conservative Weimar government.

1925

Bauhaus is re-opened in the small but expanding town of Dessau.

Pedagogical Sketchbook is published as second in a series of Bauhaus books.

Participates in first group exhibition of Surrealists in Paris.

Between 1925 and 1931, while at the Bauhaus in Dessau, produces only four etchings.

1927

Experiments with pictures scratched into a plaster ground.

1928

Essay "Exact Experiments in the Realm of Art" published by the Bauhaus.

February: Gropius resigns as Bauhaus director and is succeeded by architect Hannes Meyer.

December-January, 1928: Journey to Egypt.

10 remaining prints, from 1928-32, will be etchings.

1929

Monograph on Klee by Will Grohmann published.

Experiments with bas-relief "drawings" scratched into limestone and plaster.

1930

Retrospective in Flechtheim travels to the Museum of Modern Art, New York.

Mies van der Rohe succeeds Hannes Meyer as Bauhaus director.

Accepts a professorship at Dusseldorf Academy of Arts in order to escape the strain of working at the Bauhaus in an atmosphere hostile to painting.

1931

Officially released from Bauhaus contract, teaches fulltime in Dusseldorf. There his professional obligations are light, allowing more time to devote to his own art.

1932

Last print, zinc plate etching *Why Does He Run?,* created for a print portfolio published to benefit Christian Zervos' financially troubled *Cahiers d'Art.*

1933

Dismissed from Dusseldorf Academy by Nazi officials as part of a general effort to excise modernism from German cultural institutions.

Emigrates from Dusseldorf to Bern, where he applies for Swiss citizenship.

1934

Signs contract with art dealer Daniel Henry Kahnweiler.

First exhibition in England, at the Mayor Gallery, London.

1935

Retrospective with 237 works in Bern and Basel.

Learns he is afflicted with scleroderma.

1936

Convalescent stay in Tarasp and Montana. Depressed by illness, produces few works.

1937

17 works included in Nazi exhibition of "degenerate art" in Munich.

1938

Begins a final and extraordinarily prolific campaign of paintings and drawings.

1939

Visits an exhibition in Geneva of masterpieces from Prado Museum. Greatly admires El Greco, Goya, Bosch and Brueghel.

Angels and demons are dominating pictorial motifs from 1939-40.

1940

Large exhibition of 1935-40 works in Zurich.
29 June: Dies of scleroderma.

Memorial exhibitions in Bern, New York and, in 1941, in Basel and Zurich.

The Hero with the Wing, *1905. Etching on zinc, 257 × 160 mm. (plate). Collection of the Art Institute of Chicago. (K 16).*

Introduction to the Exhibition

By Jim Jordan

Paul Klee practiced the art of the print for over thirty years, producing a hundred and ten prints. [1] The number is not large in comparison to this prolific artist's work in the other media; and a large portion of them were done in the early part of his career, before he developed his powers as a colorist and painter. Yet, this work contains some of Klee's most fascinating images in a variety of techniques. Sixty-three of the prints are intaglios—etchings and drypoints. Forty-three are lithographs, mostly in black and white, with the exception of six which are in color. Four other lithographs, in one of Klee's most interesting variations, were painstakingly hand colored by the artist even though they were published in large editions. Klee took only a brief interest in woodcut, in contrast to most other German artists of his generation; and he completed only two prints (and two fragments) in this medium, neither of which was printed as an edition.

Klee began his printmaking career with a series of satirical intaglio prints which he called his "Inventions" created between 1903 and 1905. Here, with distorted but comparatively traditional figures, Klee commented on the hypocracies of society as he saw them. In the next few years he experimented with looser techniques, such as "*reservage*" or lift ground, and a sketchy manner of drypoint done at times on celluloid. The subjects of these were more naturalistic themes, landscapes, and occasional figures. 1912 was a year of experimentation for Klee, as evidenced by his woodcut attempts as well as his first essays in lithography. He returned in 1913 to the classic etching technique for a series of abstract proto-Cubist plates (again none of them editioned); and he continued to produce occasional etchings and drypoints during the next few years. Klee's interest in lithography developed further during this period. Major prints were produced in 1915 and 1916; and in 1919 six lithographs, with subjects ranging from a mystical self-portrait to fantasies on the evolution of insects, were done for publication in a journal of poetry and original graphics. During the early to mid-1920s, in collaboration with the craftsmen at the Bauhaus, Klee explored his interest in lithography to its fullest, producing eleven lithographs with the Bauhaus Press and a small number of others which were only carried through the proof stage. Several of these were in color and the most complex, a four-color print, was one of the postcards advertising the 1923 Bauhaus Exhibition. For his last print-making years, 1928-1932, Klee turned again to etching with variations in lift ground, *Il. 125* aquatint, and drypoint. His last print was the half-comical line drawing *Why Does He Run?* etched cleanly in zinc. Klee turned his attention thereafter, away from the print-making media.

For the present exhibition as many of Klee's prints as possible have been assembled in association with preparatory drawings, and other print-related materials. Because of the frequently unusual nature of Klee's involvement with prints, the contextual material has a special importance and its inclusion is intended to provide background and comparative material, to better place Klee's prints in the totality of his oeuvre and in the context of the printmaking of his time.

The material is displayed chronologically, with the elaboration of a section with books and group portfolios in which a number of Klee's prints appeared. There is more than the usual art-historical reason for showing his prints in chronological order. They offer, of course, an overview of his art but even more strikingly, as a series they embody a successon of styles. Klee placed great value on development, stating flatly in one aphorism that "becoming is more important than being."[2] His *Diaries* and other autobiographical writings emphasize the theme of evolution—style is seen to grow out of style as a discovery, a corrective, or advance. And the artist's career, not unlike the single work, is thought to unfold in measurable steps. Thus, as a series, the prints offer a view of Klee with several dimensions.

Early Prints, 1903-1911: One is struck by the sureness of Klee's early etchings, with the polish just as much as with the idiosyncrasy of his "Inventions," his first major statement in any medium. Klee was only a year or so out of the art academy, living again with his parents in Bern, when he began the series. Connoisseurs and scholars have long commented on the sophistication of these early works, ranking them among the outstanding prints of the Art-Nouveau-Symbolist period which produced many printmaking specialists. A number of the "Inventions" are in the exhibition, in- *Il. 15/21* cluding *Virgin in the Tree*, one of the first executed, two versions of *Comedian, Two* *Il. 19/26* *Men Meet Each Supposing the Other to be of Higher Rank, The Hero with the Wing,* *Il. 31* and *Threatening Head,* the last of the series. The message of these prints, though very complex, is clear in outline: one is trapped by the bourgeois social conventions *(Virgin)*, one suffers behind masks of various kinds *(Comedians)*, and a modern soul is unable to maintain the solemnity of an antique role (*Perseus*). Irony and frustration appear to be the themes of *Threatening Head, The Hero with the Wing,* and *Senile Phoenix*.

Max Girardet, a fine printer in Bern, pulled the small editions for Klee.[3] Given their

The Senile Phoenix, *1905. Etching on zinc, 270 × 198 mm. (plate). Collection of Professor Carl Djerassi, Stanford University. (K 17 IIb)*

traditional technique, we cannot very easily see (as we can with Klee's later, more modernistic prints) the steps by which these etchings were produced. While there are many drawings that in one way or another relate to the "Inventions," only two direct preparatory drawings (*Vorzeichnungen*) have survived.[4] The pencil drawing *The Hero with the Wing* was probably traced onto the asphaltum-grounded zinc plate by a process resembling carbon paper. This would account for the single reversal of the image between print and drawing (in contrast to the soluble reversal which occurs when a graphite drawing is offset facedown, directly onto the plate). The subtle differences here between sketch and finished version, between the hatched and stippled shadings, between the renditions of the peg-legged sprouting foot, reward close examination.[5]

As an interesting sidelight on the series dating from 1904, the year when *Pessimistic Symbol of the Mountain* and *Crown Mania* were done, is a satirical pencil drawing *Limping Girl with an Apple.* This might well have been a prelude to yet another social-critical "Invention," satirizing this time the story of Eve. It was, in fact, utilized two years later as a model for a glass painting, a medium that was at the time closely related to etching in Klee's thought and procedures.[6] The most relevant thing about the drawing however is the superimposed notations in ink, dated May 1904, of etching formulae. One formula for "quick copper etching" lists as proportional parts "5 nitric acid/2 acetic acid/3 water." The other notes are conversions into a fifth and a tenth of this recipe. It is curious that Klee would jot on a drawing so carelessly, and then still meticulously catalogue and mount it as he did all his works.[7] *Dame* or *Lady* is a lost 1904 etching (which Jurgen Glaesemer has convincingly reconstructed)[8] heavily reworked with pencil and ink a year later. The work in its present state served, in turn, as the basis for *Portrait of a Sentimental Lady,* a glass painting of 1906. The whole design, scholars have pointed out, is highly reminiscent of the Art-Nouveau illustrations of Felicien Rops or Aubrey Beardsley.[10] On the reverse of *Lady* is yet another rarity, a hand-pulled gouache impression of the nearly-forgotten relief etching *Prophet*[11] which, even in its fragmentary state, like so many of Klee's early figures, shows the influence of the Swiss painter and muralist Ferdinand Hodler.

From Klee's Impressionistic period, which followed his marriage and move to Munich in 1906, his lighter approach through a contour that (as he wrote in 1911) "gather[s] and capture[s] the impressionisms,"[12] is represented in *New Avenue—1st Version.* The standard etched line is further varied in several prints, as here in *Suburban Villas,* with a lift-ground technique. The image was drawn on the plate with a water-soluble, absorbent ink mixture swelled to burst through the varnish, and the exposed, granular lines were subsequently etched. In some of Klee's lift grounds a tonal, painterly effect results,[13] but in *Suburban Villas* the technique produces an open line that shows one more aspect of Klee's ambition of the time to adapt line to the depiction of light. A lighter touch still is exemplified in the drypoints on celluloid, such as *Steamships in Harbor.* The spontaneous plein-air effect here has again been carefully contrived, as there exist preparatory drawings for many of the drypoints just as for the more laborious techniques.[14]

Il. 48
Il. 43

Menancing Head, *1905. Etching on zinc, 200 × 145 mm. (plate). Collection of Professor Carl Djerassi, Stanford University. (K 18a)*

Through generous loans from the Paul Klee Foundation in the Kunstmuseum Bern, we have a glimpse of one of the most imaginative variations Klee did during this period. The zinc etching *Bern* was never editioned, but it has an interesting family relationship to at least three other works, two in the exhibition. As Jürgen Glaesemer
Il. 44 describes in his essay below,[15] the 1909 drawing *Bern, Industrial District of the Matte, Above it the Minster Tower, Islands of Light,* is the seminal image for the etching (which is reversed). From the same basic drawing came yet another drawing, and a glass painting in wash, all showing the dramatic view of the Bern *Alstadt* perched on a bluff above the lower section of the city along the Aare. In his diary, Klee diagrammed a method of projecting distorted images from such glass paintings,[16] and Glaesemer explains below that this is the origin of the proportional stretching of the scene in the drawing *Bern, the Matte with the Minster Rising Above, Vertical Conception.*

Prints of the Transitional Period, 1912-1916: Klee's production of 1912 totaled twelve prints comprised of the woodcuts, one drypoint, and his first nine lithographs. In-
Il. 35 cluded in the exhibition is the beautiful ink drawing *Self-Portrait, Conceived as a Woodcut* of 1910, from which surprisingly no print ever resulted. It is therefore more of a meditation on the woodcut idea, seen again from Klee's particular interest in the massed effects he called "light-forms" and "islands."[17] *Reclining Figure,* one of the woodcuts Klee actually finished in 1912, has a slightly different conception. It is a light-form of sorts where both the inner substance and the outer ground are hollowed away. The woodcut *Under the Sun* (not in the exhibition) by contrast has the rich blacks we associate with the more famous modern German woodcut artists such as Kirchner and Franz Marc. In fact it is more than likely that the print was influenced in form and imagery by Marc whom Klee had met the year before, the connection supported by the fact that the woodcut was in Marc's collection.[18]

Klee's first lithographic ventures have been the subject of much discussion, since a few years ago when Glaesemer first published Klee's letter to Alfred Kubin indicating his uneasiness with lithography.[19] In the essay reprinted below (p. 74), we read of Klee's opinion, late in 1911, that lithography was essentially a reproductive technique, useful for advertising or "propaganda," but ultimately subordinate to the freer, more autographic part of art. The first lithographs, accordingly, are not overly adven-
Il. 55 turesome, but in *Saint George* and *Tragedy on Stilts* we can see the freewheeling, open style of other 1912 drawings, such as the illustrations to Voltaire's *Candide* which were finished that year. Included in the show, as well, is *Flight to the Stars,* one of a series of thirty-six drawings done on lithographic transfer paper. They were catalogued by Klee as lithographs but never actually carried out as prints. Marcel Franciscono has recently suggested that this series may have been conceived as illustrations to Goethe's *Faust,*[20] a possibility certainly consistent with the *Candide* project. The *Candide* drawings, incidentally, lay fallow for a number of years, until they were finally published by Kurt Wolf in 1920.

In the context of Klee's drawing style, *Saint George,* along with a couple of preliminary *Candide* sketches, can be seen to embody Klee's first employment of the

Cubist fragment or facet which he was studying intensely at the time. Subsequently in 1913, he carried out a very controlled group of etchings in a pen-drawing style, in which he further explored the Cubist method of spatial structure.[21] *Pomp in Miniature*
Il. 57 and *Garden of Passion,* both in the exhibition, have a curious leaf-like style; and
Il. 65 *Abstraction II* (probably from later in the year) shows how Klee radically reduced even the cryptic imagery of the earlier two prints in his adaptation to the Cubist scaffolding. *Abstraction II* has not only the characteristic two-dimensional pattern, but also the shallow relief space of Analytic Cubism, brought about through the interlocking of tilted planes that is usually termed *passage.*[22] As a fascinating comparison to these abstract etchings, the exhibition includes a famous Klee drawing of the same
Il. 64 vintage, *Fabulous Island.* In contrast to *Abstraction II, Fabulous Island* has many tiny fragments and suggestions of figures, animal heads, tails, limbs, and claws, that peek out through the openings in the lattice. While Klee had come to understand the forms of Cubism and their interrelationship in space, he was still undecided about what consequences the new idiom might have for his playful, figure-narrative style. He appears to speculate, at least in the prints, that the adoption of Cubism might lead to abstraction, to the abandonment of all figurative elements—an idea that he had expressed in an article the year before.[23]

1914 was the year of Klee's development to maturity in the area of color, having been deeply affected by a trip to North Africa which he took with fellow artists Louis Moilliet and August Macke. His energies were focused decidedly on watercolor, as he wrote in this diary on the evening of April 16th, "Color possesses me . . . That is the meaning of this happy hour: Color and I are one. I am a painter."[24] Not surprisingly his interest in prints waned for the moment, and he produced only four prints during the year. Klee's coloristic achievement of 1914 also embraced the final terms of the Cubist reconstruction of his work. The conflict between the tiny figures, and the abstract gridwork was resolved by enlarging the figurative elements up to the same scale as the linear framework. Klee composed his paintings, drawings, and prints henceforth on this Cubist basis until the late 1920s.[25] An example of the further development of this style is the beautiful hand-colored lithograph *Destruction and Hope,* which Klee finished late in 1916.

Prints of the Post-War and Bauhaus Years, 1918-1932: Klee's prints enter another new context at this point as, beginning in 1912 and with greater frequency toward the end of the decades, they appeared in journals of original graphics, deluxe editions, and group portfolios. A collection of such publications makes up a major feature of this
Il. 63 exhibition: Klee contributed two prints, *Battlefield* and *Death for the Idea,* to the "war-diary" publication *Zeit-Echo,* where they constitute (as O. K. Werckmeister has pointed
Il. 73 out)[26] his most direct public comment on the war. Six lithographs *(Three Heads,*
Il. 83 *Acrobats, Number-Tree Landscape, Meditation,* and *The Horrible Dream* and *Insects)*
85/86 appeared on the pages of the poetry and graphics journal, *Münchner Blätter für Dichtung und Graphik.* Klee contributed as well to *Das Kestnerbuch,* of 1919, which contains work by eleven other artists, and to the 1920 *Deutsche Graphiker der Gegenwart,* which includes among its eighteen contributors, Barlach, Beckmann, Feininger,

Kollwitz, and Grosz as well. There are other publications of the kind which are not included in the exhibition.[27]

From our historical point of view the appeal of such compilations is obvious. They offer us opportunities to view the artist's work in the context of its original publications with the ideological "package" surrounding the work still intact. We may read the associated texts in the journals, and examine the stylistic programs and conflicts embodied by the anthologies of art. Even when prints such as Klee's have been abstracted from the journals and portfolios to stand alone as independent works, they can only gain in additional meaning when considered again in their original context.

As Christian Geelhaar has emphasized in his 1974 article reprinted below,[28] making prints to appear in books may well correspond to the applied-art aspect of the medium that Klee so mistrusted. This lack of enthusiasm may also account for the
Il. 59 discontinuity in the origin of some of the print images. *Small World,* for example, was
Il. 57 five years old when it appeared in *Die Schaffenden,* and *Garden of Passion* of 1913 was resurrected after five years for a second edition which was distributed as a supplement to *Expressionisms,* a book by Herwarth Walden.[29]

The preparatory drawings for *Acrobats* and *Number-Tree Landscape,* in the exhibition, reveal some detailed aspects of Klee's "applied" lithography. The drawing for *Number-Tree Landscape* was duplicated in the print with great fidelity. Dating from 1918, it appears to have been an actual scratch sheet from Klee's days in the army as a paymaster's assistant, only slightly modified to form the image of a landscape. Most of the columns of numbers actually add up correctly, despite their transformation by the artist into trees and branches. The pencil line is closely followed in the pen-lithograph, and most amazing of all, the fuzzy, irregular border of the drawing is scrupulously copied in the print. *Acrobats* was handled differently, with Klee taking more obvious advantage, or at least cognizance, of the manipulative opportunities offered by the transfer onto the stone. In the print he has cut off, either by masking or erasing, a strip across the bottom which contained the juggler's feet in the drawing. He has also omitted in the print one of the legs of the topmost figure. Klee has subtlely modified the smudges and lines to change the effect from a single large figure to two interlocked figures at the base of the print.

It is possible that Klee thought of this series of lithographs as reproductions, somewhere between the purely mechanical facsimile and the hand-done original. He was, between 1919-1920, much involved with reproductive technique. His *Candide* drawings were finally reproduced by a photomechanical process, as were his 1918-1919 illustrations to Curt Corrinth's *Potsdamer Platz.* And on the occasion of a Klee exhibition in 1920, the dealer Hans Goitz published a 300-copy facsimile-lithograph of Klee's 1914 watercolor *Park* [30] (examples of the foregoing are in the exhibition). The quality of the photoreproductions is high, and it is certainly possible that Klee did not at this point think of the various duplicative processes as very far apart.

With the group portfolios included in the exhibition, we see Klee among artistic contemporaries with whom he had varying relationships, and we may examine some

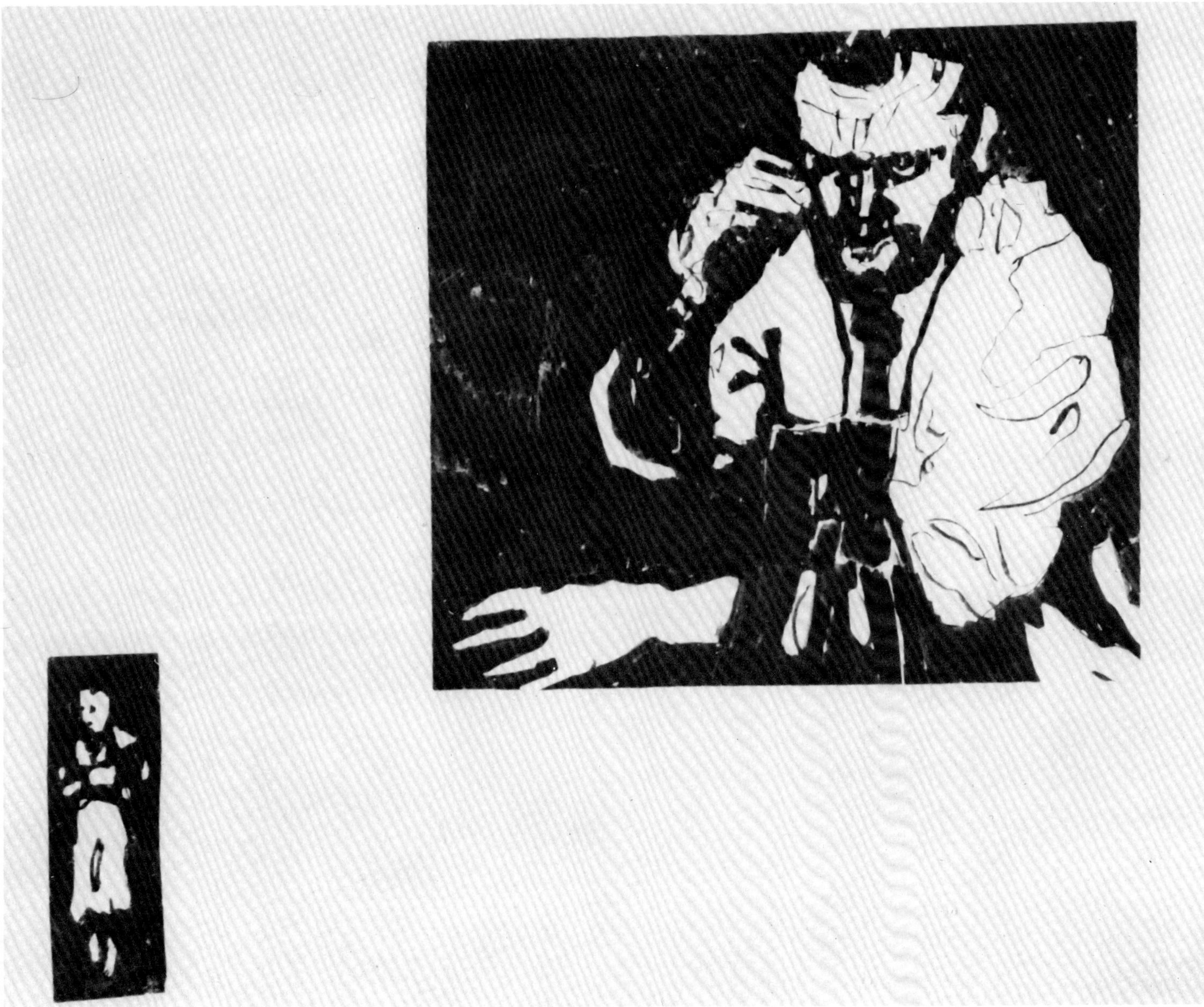

Self Portrait, (Conceived as a Woodcut), *1909.*
Pen and ink, 168 × 240 mm. Collection of Felix Klee. Bern, Switzerland. (1909.39B)

of the themes that bound such groups together. The institution of group portfolios was probably more common in Germany than any other country. One thinks, for example, of the *Brücke* group's annual portfolios with prints by all of the members. Such publications had a number of functions: stylistically they consolidated and documented the artists' work and progress, and they disseminated their work more widely than paintings. Profit from the sale of a portfolio might benefit the group, or even another recipient,[31] but the institution probably functioned in many cases more as artistic-social "glue" than as a profit-making venture. Subscriptions for portfolios offered friends a way to participate in a movement. Manifestos sometimes appeared with the prints (the *Brücke* portfolios again are the primary model), as well as lists of "active and passive" members. Passive members were sympathetic, often influential people who wanted to identify with the spirit of the group endeavor. Such a list for example made up part of the machinery of the *Moderner Bund* portfolio, in which Klee participated.[32]

Klee's first group venture was with the large association called *SEMA* ("The Sign"), which also included the expressionistic writer and illustrator Alfred Kubin. Their portfolio of fifteen original lithographs (the topic of Klee's letter) appeared in 1912 with
Il. 53/57 Klee's *View on a River.* Klee next published his *Garden of Passion* (for its first edition) in the smaller, 1913 portfolio of the Swiss association of artists, the *Moderner Bund.* He had already exhibited earlier with this group (which included the young Hans Arp), and had written a now-famous review of their 1912 exhibition.[33]

Two later portfolios, the first folder of *Die Schaffenden,* and the Bauhaus Press's *Nue Europaische Graphik: Erste Mappe: Meister des Staatlichen Bauhauses in Weimar* offer a broad perspective on the crucial post-World War I period. The first of those appeared in 1919, the second in 1921. *Die Schaffenden* puts Klee in the demanding context of the outstanding Expressionists of the day: Erich Heckel , Paula Modersohn-Becker, Max Pechstein, Karl Schmidt-Rottluff, and others. Klee had had earlier contacts with Expressionism he had shown with Walden's *Sturm,* he knew Expressionist writers, and the famous *Blaue Reiter* group with which he was associated had included prints by the *Brücke* artists in its 1912 graphic exhibition.[34] But this portfolio provides us with one of our only direct comparisons of Klee to the Expressionistic
Il. 59 mainstream. His *Small World* seems particularly miniature-like in this company. This etching is not typical of Klee's work of 1919, it had in fact been made in 1914, but its imagery of leering heads, tumbling figures, and its rugged technique may have suggested to Klee that it be appropriate for the context. Some observers have described *Small Worlds* as primitive and chaotic,[35] and emotional content of this kind might qualify it as Expressionistic, though to be sure, it looks a bit timid next to the bold woodcuts of Schmidt-Rottluff.

The Bauhaus portfolio, by contrast, contains two of the strongest prints in all of Klee's oeuvre. This was the first portfolio of an ambitious Bauhaus campaign of documentation, in prints, of contemporary modernism from all the major countries.[36]
Il. 91/40 Klee's *Saint of the Inner Light* and *Hoffmannesque Scene* appear here along with two works apiece by the other Bauhaus masters, Lionel Feininger, Johannes Itten, Gerhard

Three Girls in the Meadow, *1910. Etching on copper, 144 × 118 mm. Collection of Kunstmuseum, Bern, Switzerland. (K 28)*

Marcks, George Muche, Oskar Schlemmer, and Lothar Schreyer. These comparisons give a fascinating survey not only of the Bauhaus faculty of the early Weimar years, but of a type of romantic-mystical style, a successor to the pre-war *Blaue Reiter* style, which flourished in Germany in the early twenties. Itten's *Saying* and Muche's *Etching: One Hand, Two Hearts Over a Chessboard,* are examples, which draw upon the same mythologizing, occult fund of imagery as the two Klees. These artists moreover compose their mysterious effects in the same way, grouping them loosely around a geometric armature. The comparison in turn emphasizes the confident mastery that Klee enjoyed by 1921 as a long-time veteran in this idiom.

Klee's prints of the Bauhaus years are marvels of balance between the fantastic and
Il. 91 the rational, as befit his concept of the Bauhaus ideal.[37] In *Saint of the Inner Light,*
the human form, the cranium, the features, the breast, are subjected to a geometric rule as strict as a medieval doctrine. The head is thus framed by chords of a halo-circle, and the mouth and eyes are reduced to branches of a facial stem. The coloration of rose and tan adds a paradoxical richness, and forms a tonal context that
Il. 93 makes the figure seem to glow. *Hoffmannesque Scene* suggests, with small puppet or
stage figures, the sort of psychological tale for which the writer E.T.A. Hoffmann is famous. Yellow and violet color stones overlay in this lithograph, producing a third color of brown on certain squares, the most complex and at the same time economical color effect in all of Klee's prints. These lithographs are fully the equal of Klee's most elaborate paintings of the twenties.

Most of Klee's lithographs of the 1920s were printed at the Bauhaus, and four of
Il. 112 them were part of other group endeavors: *Man in Love* figured in the 1923 *Meister-*
Il. 111 *mappe des Staatlichen Bauhauses;* and *Bauhaus Lantern Festival, The Exalted Side,* and
The Livelier Side were published to celebrate communal events—a summer solstice festival, and the occasion of a major 1923 exhibition held by the school, for which other artists also did postcards. Preparatory drawings exist from most periods of Klee's print production. However those from 1919 through the early Bauhaus period have a special interest. While working on the transfer lithographic process in 1919, Klee apparently hit upon the procedure of tracing his drawings, by the use of a handmade "carbon" paper, onto the transfer paper.[38] The transfer then, in a standard procedure, was placed face down and offset onto the prepared lithographic stone by the press. Two advantages were secured: the image having been reversed only once came out on the print with the same orientation as the drawing.[39] And the drawing, since it had been merely traced over with a sharp stylus, was unaltered by the process and could even be reemployed as a guide for later transfers. Drawings and watercolors, usually called oil-transfer paintings, were made by the same procedure. Some of the
Il. 97 prints derived from this process, such as *Tightrope Walker* and *The Singer of the*
Comic Opera, exist as versions in the other media. The preparatory drawings in the present exhibition for *Saint of the Inner Light* and *The Exalted Side* are fine examples
Il. 95 of the first stage of the transfer process. The transfer procedure for *Steamer before*
Il. 109 *Lugano* and *The Witch with the Comb* is less obvious. However it was carried out, it
did not generate the informal, accidental smudges that are typical of the "carbon"

paper technique; and as a consequence, these prints foreshadow Klee's clean-lined style of the later twenties.[40]

Klee's last ten prints dating from 1928 to 1932 are all etchings, and in some ways they appear traditional compared to what had come before. There are line etchings such as *Old Men Figuring,* and combinations involving aquatint, as in *Never Ending,* all with a polish we have not seen in Klee's intaglios since the early "Inventions." The preparatory drawings as well are not so directly related to the prints as with the lithographs. The beautiful pen drawing for *L'Homme Approximatif,* as Geelhaar has well pointed out,[41] is an independent work in another medium by no means subsequent to the print—indeed, probably, superior to it. If there is a sense of great "finish" in these prints, they nevertheless involved changes. The two states of *Girl's Head*, for example, differ quite a bit. In the early version,[42] the contours of the face were formed by masses of sketchy hair to the sides and top of the head. In the final revision these scraped, fuzzy patterns have been burnished out and replaced by the firm, unbroken contours of the face. The open head is closed by the serrated crown, and the eyes are joined by a "stem" which passed through the bridge of the nose. The eyebrows likewise meld into a continuous line from temple to temple, exemplifying Klee's late-twenties interest in complete, closed contours, very different in feeling from the sketchier approximations of his Cubist years.[43]

Il. 121

Il. 123

The matter of the hand colored prints is one of the most fascinating of Klee's oeuvre. The early hand-coloration and stencil procedures of *Destruction and Hope, Insects,* and *A Genius Serves a Little Breakfast* were superceded in the twenties by the two and three-color lithographs. In the most elaborate of these such as *Hoffmannesque Scene* and *The Loftier Side,* Klee must have felt a great satisfaction. Here he achieved almost the richness of full-color painting, while still utilizing the graphic elements in a way that is very print-like, by no means a mere reproduction. The earlier hand-colored proof of *The Loftier Side* is instructive in this regard being clearly a field of planning for the four-color print which followed.

Il. 66

Il. 106/107

Il. 93

Il. 111

Other prints, such as the very beautiful *Striding Figures* and *Collapsing,* may be watercolor sketches planned for further development in color lithography.[44] And yet, as Glaesemer and others have well noted, these hand-painted combinations are extremely painting-like, really a hybrid medium.[45] Even Klee's inscription on the hand-colored vesion of *Collapsing* notes methodically that the 1923 lithograph had been watercolored in 1926, and the result was mounted as a watercolor.[46] Like the several beautifully hand-colored copies of *Singer of the Comic Opera* (not in the show),[47] *Collapsing* was tinted with an atomizer, which produced a mysterious, color-laden atmosphere in which the linear image seems suspended. The rich *Comic Opera* prints were, as scholars have noted, special gifts for members of the support group, the Klee Society.[48]

Il. 97

Il. 86

Finally, the *Meditation-Self-Portrait,* another print with a hand-colored version, has a special role in our picture of Klee. Self-portraits hold a continuous fascination for this artist, particularly during introspective periods. He did other self-portraits in 1919, and it has even been observed that there is something self-portrait-like in most of Klee's heads, particularly when they represent creators or performers.[49] But this self-portrait depicts the artist in a specific way that makes two major references. First one might note the internal structure of the features, which are treated as an early form of the leaf-and-stem face, and which have, it has been also suggested, sexual analogies as well.[50] The image is a veritable model for the botanical image of the artist which Klee put forth six years after the print. In his well-known *Jenaer Kunstverein* lecture, he likens the artist to a tree through which art "flows"—from the source in the roots to the flowering in the work which, miraculously, is almost beyond the artist's personal understanding.[51] But in addition we may see here the unmistakable image of the artist as Buddha, or at least as a tonsured, meditative monk whose eyes are serenely shut to the outer world, his gaze turned inward toward mystical reality.[52] Almost, one might propose, as if to personalize this image—which appeared otherwise in the large edition of a journal. Klee hand-colored at least a single copy which has survived in the legacy-collection of his son Felix Klee. Here clearly a print has been reclaimed by the art of painting, as Klee's most evocative self-portrait is elaborated, turned almost into an icon through color. For Paul Klee the borders between painting and prints, as well as those among the other media, were never static, never restrictive, and his movement in and out of prints over the years is the subject for a separate meditation.

FOOTNOTES

1. One hundred nine prints are listed in the standard catalogue, Eberhard W. Kornfeld, *Verzeichnis der graphischen Werkes von Paul Klee* (Bern: Verlag Kornfeld und Klipstein, 1963). (Prints are often identified by their Kornfeld numbers.) The heavily reworked etching *Dame* is usually catalogued as the drawing *Critique of Normal Woman* (see Jürgen Glaesemer, *Paul Klee: Handzeichnungen I: Kindheit bis 1920* (Bern: Kunstmuseum Bern, 1973), no. 291; also see references, Jim M. Jordan, "Prints and Oil-Transfer Work," p. 103, n. 2 below).

2. Paul Klee, *The Diaries of Paul Klee, 1898-1918,* Edited, with an Introduction, by Felix Klee (Berkeley: University of California Press, 1964), no. 924 (1914).

3. Information on the printers and publishers of Klee's prints is given in Kornfeld, *Verzeichnis.*

4. Preparatory drawings are known for *The Hero with the Wing* and *Pessimistic Symbol of the Mountain* (ibid., for a list of preparatory drawings).

5. Mark Rosenthal briefly discusses the comparison in "Der Held mit dem Flügel': Zur Metapher des Fluges im Werk von Paul Klee," in Wilhelm-Lehmbruck-Museum der Stadt

Duisburg, *Paul Klee: Das graphische und plastische Werk,* Exhibition October 20, 1974—January 1, 1975, p. 30.

6. Glaesemer, *Handzeichnungen I,* no. 288.

7. For a general description of Klee's oeuvre-catalogue, see Felix Klee, Paul Klee, Paul Klee: *His Life and Work in Documents* (New York: Braziller, 1962), pp. 201-203.

8. Jürgen Glaesemer, " 'Die Kritik des Normalweibes': Zu Form und Inhalt im Frühwerk von Paul Klee," in Wilhelm-Lehmbruck-Museum Duisburg, *Klees graphisches Werk,* p. 41; also Glaesemer, *Handzeichnungen I,* no. 291.

9. Jurgen Glaesemer, *Paul Klee: The Colored Works in the Kunstmuseum Bern* (Bern: Kuntsmuseum Bern, 1979), no. 13.

10. Glaesemer, "Die Kritik des Normalweibes," p. 42; Jim M. Jordan, "Paul Klee and Cubism, 1912-1926," 2 vols. (Ph.D. dissertation, Institute of Fine Arts, New York University, 1974; Ann Arbor, Michigan: University Microfilms), pp. 24-28. This material also appears on pp. 13-16 of my revised dissertation, shortly to appear as *Paul Klee and Cubism* (Princeton, N.J.: Princeton University Press, forthcoming). All future references here will be to this later book.

11. Published in Glaesemer, "Kritik des Normalweibes," pp. 40-41 (an earlier version of this essay appeared in *Berner Mitteilungen* [Bern], nos. 131/132 [January/February 1972], pp. 2-13).

12. Klee, *Diaries,* no. 894.

13. As an example, *Drinker* (Kornfeld no. 21), not included in the exhibition.

14. Kornfeld, *Verzeichnis.*

15. Jürgen Glaesemer, "Paul Klee's Prints," p. 72 below.

16. Klee, *Diaries,* no. 892 (1911).

17. Ibid., no. 874 (1910), for Klee's definition of light-forms.

18. Information about Marc's collection from Kornfeld, no. 51.

19. Glaesemer, "Klee's Prints," p. 74 below.

20. Marcel Franciscono, "Paul Klee's Lithographic Drawings of 1912: Some Unexpected Illustrations of 'Faust'," *Pantheon* 41, no. 1 (January-March 1983): 34-38.

21. For a discussion of the Cubistic drawings and etchings of 1913, see Jordan, *Paul Klee and Cubism,* pp. 105-115.

22. Ibid., esp. p. 109.

23. Paul Klee, "Die Ausstellung des Modernen Bundes im Kunsthaus Zürich," *Die Alpen* (Bern), Jhrg. VI, Heft 12 (August 1912), pp. 696-704 (as reprinted in Christian Geelhaar, ed., *Paul Klee Schriften: Rezensionen und Aufsätze* [Cologne: DuMont, 1976] pp. 105-111, esp. 107-108).

24. Klee, *Diaries,* no. 926 (Thursday, April 17, 1914).

25. Jordan, *Paul Klee and Cubism,* passim; the latter part of Chapter 8 is concerned with the end of Klee's Cubist period in the late 1920s.

26. O. K. Werckmeister, "Klee im Ersten Weltkrieg," in Städtische Galerie im Lenbachhaus, Munchen, *Paul Klee: Das Frühwerk: 1883-1922,* Exhibition December 12, 1979—March 2, 1980, pp. 166-171.

27. Others are listed in Kornfeld, *Verzeichnis;* for example, *A Genuis Serves a Little Breakfast* (Kornfeld no. 79 II. c.) appeared in a hand-colored edition of 50 in *"Die Freude": Blätter einer neuen Gesinnung,* Vol. 1 (1920), published by Wilhelm Uhde (Burg Lauenstein, Oberfranken).

28. Christian Geelhaar, "Paul Klee's Graphic Small World: 1912-1932," p. 58 below.

29. Kornfeld no. 56. e.

30. Regarding the photomechanical reproductions of the *Candide* drawings, see Glaesemer, *Handzeichnungen I,* pp. 183-184; the reproductions for *Postdamer Platz,* ibid., p. 257, n. 15; and the facsimile-lithograph of *Park,* Kornfeld no. A112 (appendix).

31. See Geelhaar, "Klee's Graphic Small World," p. 50 n. 47 below, for an example of a portfolio with a beneficiary.

32. Description, Kornfeld no. 56. c.

33. See note 23 above

34. A convenient reprint of the Blaue Reiter Exhibition Catalogues, with the original illustrations, appears in Rosel Golek, *Der Blaue Reiter im Lenbachhaus München* (Munich: Prestel-Verlag, 1982), pp. 404-413. Klee's

Diaries report an exhibition and dealings with Walden's *Sturm* in 1917 (for example, nos. 1062, 1064, 1066), and potential collaboration with the Expressionist writer Theodor Däubler in 1918 (nos. 1100, 1114, 1126a).

35. Marcel Franciscono, "Paul Klee's kubistische Druckgraphik." in Wilhelm-Lehmbruck-Museum Duisburg, *Klees graphisches Werk,* p. 53.

36. See Geelhaar, "Klee's Graphic Small World," p. 52 below, for a review of this project.

37. Among Klee's many writings of the Bauhaus years, probably his clearest statement about the balancing of rationality and intuition is the essay "Exact Experiments in the Realm of Art" (*Exakte Versuche im Bereiche der Kunst),* first published in *Bauhaus, Vierteljahrzeitschrift für Gestaltung* (Dessau), vol. 2, no. 2; and reprinted from the manuscript in Jürg Spiller, ed., *Paul Klee Notebooks: Volume 1: The Thinking Eye* (London: Lund Humphries, 1961), pp. 69-70.

38. See Glaesemer, "Klee's Prints," p. 72 below; as well as my essay on the topic, p. 94 below.

39. Charles W. Haxthausen notes (in "Klee, the Reluctant Printmaker," in Stanford University Museum of Art, *In Celebration of Paul Klee: 1879-1940: Fifty Prints* (Stanford Art Book 18), Catalogue of the Exhibition by Betsy G. Fryberger, Exhibition September 25—November 4, 1979, p. 11 and n. 10) that *Man in Love* (Kornfeld no. 94), as an exception, must have been traced directly onto the stone since its image is reversed from the preparatory drawing.

40. For a discussion of Klee's transition to a transparent, Constructivistic style in the late twenties, see Jordan, *Paul Klee and Cubism.* Chapter. 8.

41. Geelhaar, "Klee's Graphic Small World," p. 0 below.

42. The earlier state, described in Kornfeld (no. 101.1), is illus. in Stanford Museum, *In Celebration of Klee: Fifty Prints, no. 45.*

43. The states of *Girl's Head* are discussed in the broader context of Klee's stylistic changes of the twenties in Jordan, *Paul Klee and Cubism,* p. 187.

44. Kornfeld (nos 91 and 93) suggests this, based presumably on the very small number of impressions pulled of each.

45. Glaesemer, "Klee's Prints," p. 72 below.

46. Information from Kornfeld (no. 93).

47. Kornfled no. 99. b, lists five tinted copies; see also Geelhaar, "Klee's Graphic Small World," p. 56 and below p. 58. In the original publication of Geelhaar's essay (in Lehmbruch-Museum Duisburg, *Klees graphisches Werk)* four additional, non-print versions of the composition were illustrated.

48. Kornfeld no. 99. b.

49. Christian Geelhaar, *Paul Klee and the Bauhaus* (Greenwich, Conn.: New York Graphic Society, 1973), pp. 77-80, notes that the *Self-Portrait* hand-puppet of 1922 was Klee's last real self-portrait. He suggests that self-portraits were done during the introspective period of the *Diaries* (through 1918) as another facet of Klee's self-analysis and development; Geelhaar does note however that after this period "faces in his work occasionally still reveal personal features . . .": David R. Burnett, "Klee as Senecio: Self-Portraits 1908-1922," *Art International,* 21, no. 6 (December 1977): 12-18, discusses *Meditation* in the context of other self-portraits of 1919, and explores both the hand-puppet and *Senecio* of 1922 as metaphorical self-images.

50. Siegfried Gohr, "Symbolische Grundlagen der Kunst Paul Klees," in Kunsthalle Köln, *Paul Klee: Das Werk de Jahre 1919-1933,* Exhibition April 11—June 4. 1979, p. 84.

51. The Jena Kunstverein Lecture is reprinted, among other places, in Felix Klee, *Paul Klee,* pp. 168-179, esp. 169.

52. See Jim M. Jordan, "Garten der Mysterien: Die Ikonographie von Paul Klees expressionistischer Periode," in Lenbachhaus, *Klee Das Frühwerk,* p. 237; Margaret Plant, *Paul Klee: Figures and Faces* (London: Thames and Hudson, 1978), pp. 34-36 and nn., presents other interpretations of this lithograph based on psychoanalytic and perceptual-psychology literature.

Suburban Villas, *1910. Etching on zinc, 113 × 228 mm. Collection of Kunstmuseum, Bern, Switzerland. (K 27)*

Bern, The Industrial Part of the Matte, *1909. Pen, brush, and ink, 217 × 255 mm. Collection of Kunstmuseum, Bern, Switzerland. (1909.50)*

Bern, The Matte With the Minster Rising Above, *1910. Pen and ink, 173 × 151 mm. Collection of Kunstmuseum, Bern, Switzerland. (1910.50)*

Bern, *1910. Etching on zinc, 107 × 148 mm.*
Collection of Kunstmuseum, Bern, Switzerland. (K 32)

Munich Railway Station II, 1911. Pen & ink, 91 × 196 mm. Collection of Kunstmuseum, Bern, Switzerland. (1911.25[B])

Railroad Station, *1911. Drypoint, 148 × 198 mm. Collection of Städtische Galerie im Lenbachhaus, Munich, West Germany. (K 37a)*

New Avenue—First Version, *1910. Etching, 152 × 117 mm.*
Collection of Felix Klee, Bern, Switzerland. (K 22)

Paul Klee's Small Graphic World: 1912-1932*

By Christian Geelhaar

In the late autumn of 1922 a set of twelve original prints by Wassily Kandinsky appeared under the title *Little Worlds.* The series is composed of four lithographs, four woodcuts and four dry-point etchings.[1] Six of these works are monochrome, printed in black and on a white ground.[2] The other six are polychromatic.[3] All twelve prints were generated by a concept which permeates Kandinsky's entire oeuvre: *Little Worlds* are to be understood as metaphors for the macrocosm.

The choice of printing techniques and the alternation between monochrome and polychrome imply a didactic intention, the methodical and theoretical discussion of which was proposed by Kandinsky in his Bauhaus Book, *Point and Line to Plane.*[4] Here the artist determined specific characteristics which belong to the techniques of etching, woodcut and lithography, and explored their corresponding use in relation to the basic pictorial elements of point, line and plane. For the woodcut, an old German technique rediscovered at the beginning of the century, the basic means of expression is the plane.[5] Etching produces sharp lines[6] and also the precisest point.[7] Kandinsky considers lithography the process most appropriate for the "spirit of our times" and he praises the technique for its "facility of execution"[8] and "speed of production." "Point, line, plane, black and white, color values—everything is achieved with the highest economy."[9] Finally, he attributes the printing techniques' "social" characteristics: "The etching is undoubtedly of an aristocratic nature: it can produce only a small number of first-rate pulls which, moreover, turn out differently each time, so that every print is unique. Woodcut is more generous and egalitarian, but

**Reprinted from the exhibition catalogue at the Wilhelm-Lehmbruck Museum der Stadt Duisburg, West Germany. "Paul Klee-das graphische und plastische Werk," October 20, 1974 to January 5, 1975. Translated by Melanie Feit and Jeffrey Weiss. Reprinted with permission of the author.*

adapted only with difficulty to the use of color. Lithography on the other hand is capable of turning out an almost unlimited number of prints at top speed in a purely mechanical manner. By the constantly developing employment of color, it increasingly approximates the hand-painted picture, and it even provides a kind of substitute for painting. This clearly indicates the democratic nature of lithography."[10] Contrary to Kandinsky, and so far as can be determined on the basis of the surviving record, Paul Klee was not concerned with questions of the printmaking techniques in his Bauhaus teaching. When one surveys the prints from Klee's middle period, they give a disparate impression, only an inadequate idea of Klee's master achievements in painting and drawing from that time. Next to the metaphorical microcosm of Kandinsky's *Little Worlds,* Paul Klee's graphic works appear to borrow the title of one of his own etchings as literally a "Little World."

Paul Klee's prints from the Munich and Bauhaus periods are almost always occasional in nature. Those published originated in definite commissions as supplements to journals and deluxe editions of books, as well as contributions to collective portfolios.[11] The artist considered prints less as an opportunity to "democratize" his works for a wider audience than as a means to publicize his creative work.[12]

Of special biographical interest is a list of the places where Klee's prints were published and distributed. Paul Klee's participation in published portfolios after 1911 clearly testifies to his desire to end his periods of work in isolation and to establish contact with sympathetic minds.[13] During the autumn of 1911 a group of young painters, sculptors, and poets formed an assocation in Munich under the name of *Sema,* "The Sign." For Klee, one of the founding members, this was "a sign that I was, after all, not to remain isolated in the outside world—a timid initial attempt to join others."[14] Published in 1912 by the Delphin Press in Munich, the *Sema* portfolio contained 15 original lithographs by Karl Caspar, Robert Genin, Alfred Kubin, Max Oppenheimer, Edwin Scharff, Egon Schiele and others, including Klee's lithograph *View on a River.*[15] *Il. 53* From the beginning Klee had missed an inner unity in the *Sema* association. It was therefore not long until the news spread among the "Semists": "Klee is riding away in blue."[16] That is, he had joined his new friends Wassily Kandinsky and Franz Marc, the founders of the *Blaue Reiter* group, and had participated with 17 works in the *Blaue Reiter* black and white exhibition which opened on February 12, 1912 in the new bookshop gallery of Hans Goltz. With this step, Klee succeeded in joining the circle of the most promising German, French and Russian artists. At this second *Blaue Reiter* show, along with French Fauves, Cubists, and German painters of the *Brücke,* there were also representatives from the Swiss *Moderner Bund,* Hans Arp, Wilheim Gimmi, Walter Helbig, and Oscard Lüthy. Thereafter, in July, Klee exhibited at the Kunsthaus in Zurich with its Swiss avant-garde association. On this occasion he was welcomed by the *Moderner Bund* "as if I were already a great man" but he could not help adding: "How relative all ideas are!"[17] For the second portfolio of prints published by the *Moderner Bund* in 1913 with works by Gimmi, Helbig, Hermann Huber and Lüthy, Klee contributed a masterly etching *Garden of Passion,* *Il. 57* in the volume Expressionism of the publication *Die Kunstwende* edited by Herwarth Walden in his own Sturm press.[18] a print which would later appear in a second edition in 1918.

At the beginning of 1914 Klee was a founding member of the *Neue Münchener Sezession,* to which the art historian Wilhelm Hausenstein also belonged. In 1914, in his book *Die bildende Kunst der Gerfenwart,* Hausenstein was the first to discuss Klee in the context of a general survey of contemporary art.[19] Only in 1919, after the war, did the collective portfolio entitled 25 *Originallithographien der Münchener Neuen Sezession* appear. It included, along with Klee's curious lithograph *Bird Comedy,*[20] prints by Th. Heine, Kubin, Max Pechstein, A.H. Pellegrini, Scharff and others.

From two other contributions by Klee to print portfolios, it becomes clear that the artist had reached the forefront of the contemporary art scene in Germany in the first years after the war, and that he now belonged to the most important pioneers of the
Il. 59 avant-garde. Klee's 1914 etching *Little World* had been included in the first portfolio of the first number of the magazine for modern graphics, *Die Schaffenden,* founded and edited by Paul Westheim and published between 1919 and 1922 by Gustav Kiepenheuer in Weimar. This publication brought together prints by the most important German expressionists and French masters.[21] Finally, Klee's name appeared as a contributor to an anthology edited by Kurt Pfister in 1920, entitled *Deutsche Graphiker der Gegenwart,* along with artists such as Barlach, Beckmann, Campendonk, Corrinth, Feininger, Grosz, Heckel, Kokoschka, Kollwitz, Kubin, Liebermann, Meidner, Otto Müller, Pechstein, Rohlfs, Schmidt-Rottluf and Slevogt.[22]

In 1920 Klee's success began to mount extraordinarily. Klee's first theoretical essay *Creative Credo* was published; Curt Wolff published *Candide* with Klee's illustrations from 1912; Georg Müller, whose *Münchner Blätter für Dichtung and Graphik* in 1919
Il. 89 had already included six lithographs by Klee,[23] published the novel *Potsdamer Platz* by Curt Corrinth with Klee's illustrations. Excellent monographs by Leopold Zahn, H. von Wedderkop and Wilhelm Hausenstein evaluated Klee's artistic work. In May and June, 1920 Hans Goltz presented a broad retrospective exhibition of Klee's works to date. Besides 355 paintings, watercolors, drawings and sculptures, a large group of 27 prints could be seen in this exhibition for the first time.[24] Finally, in October of that year, Walter Gropius invited Klee to join the faculty of the Bauhaus in Weimar.[25]

"The aim of all creative activity is building." This was announced in the founding manifesto and program of the Bauhaus in April 1919.[26] The gap between fine arts and applied arts was to be overcome and, following the example of medieval Bauhutten on guilds, a unification of art and craft would contribute to a total achievement. "And this great integral work of art, this cathedral of the future, will then irradiate the smallest aspect of daily life with the intensity of its light."[27] This credo of the founder was symbolized in Lyonel Feininger's woodcut *Cathedral,*[28] which decorated the pamphlet with Gropius' manifesto.

But the "cathedral of the future" could not be built and the total work of art, ostensibly the crowning of the Bauhaus pedagogical program, was not even realized on paper. During its first years the Bauhaus did not, in fact, have an architecture department. The communal collaborative effect only occurred in other fields, such as the publication of portfolios of prints and Bauhaus books. Six printed works by Klee owe their creation to such collective undertakings.

The print workshop of the Bauhaus, with Feininger as artistic director and Carl Zaubitzer as technical expert, produced between 1921 and 1924 a great number of single prints and several print series executed by Bauhaus masters and students, as well as by outside artists.[29] The most important portfolios by painters of the Bauhaus were the *Twelve Woodcuts* by Feininger,[30] Kandinsky's *Little Worlds* (which were published by the Propyläen Press of Berlin), *Game with Heads* by Oskar Schlemmer and the woodcut illustration by Gerhard Marcks for Simrock's *Wielandslied der älteren Edda.* Prints by the eight Bauhaus masters, Feininger, Kandinsky, Klee, Marcks, Muche, Moholy-Nagy, Schlemmer, and Schreyer, were collected in the *Meistermappe des Staatlichen Bauhauses Weimar,* which appeared in 1923 as an edition of the Bauhaus Press, founded expressly for the publication of artistic prints.[31]

The most ambitious enterprise of the Bauhaus printing workshop was the portfolio series, *Neue Europäische Graphik.*[32] As Feininger remarked in a letter of November 14, 1921,[33] this work was thought of as a "creation in honor of our cause" and should document for the public "how our current generation of artists contributes towards the aims of the Bauhaus."[24] At the same time it would present the collector with "the opportunity to acquire an international collection of graphic works of fundamental importance in which Germany, France, the Netherlands, Italy, and Russia are represented by their most distinguished artists," which, due to economic circumstances, would otherwise be impossible. The announcement of the projected five-part portfolio names 75 artists who agreed to donate their prints to the Bauhaus; hardly anyone with an influential name during the twenties was missing. Inflation, scarce resources, and defective organization and coordination frequently threatened the realization of this magnificent project and necessitated significant modifications of the original plan. Only four of the projected five portfolios actually appeared. In 1922, portfolio numbers I, *Meister des Staalichen Bauhauses Weimar,*[35] *and III, Deutsche Küntsler,* were produced. The fifth, with a second series of works by German artists, followed in March 1923. The distribution of portfolio IV, *Italienische und russische Künstler,* was only begun at the beginning of 1924. The second portfolio, orginally conceived for prints of French artists, remained a fragment and was not published.

Not only were most editions of the prints pulled at the Bauhaus Press, but the Masters were also entrusted with the layout of the portfolios. Feininger designed the lettering of the press information edition notation, and tables of contents. He also produced a woodcut for the cover of the first portfolio.[36] The Bauhaus colophon, designed by Oskar Schlemmer, was placed underneath the press information. The bookbinding work was executed by the bookbindery, which, belonging to the famous master Otto Dorfner, was annexed by the Bauhaus as a teaching workshop between 1919 and 1922. Paul Klee presided as artistic director over the bookbindery.[37] The design of the cover paper of the third portfolio executed in the glue print process has

View on a River, *1912. Lithograph, c. 197 × 285 mm. (composition). Collection of Professor Carl Djerassi, Stanford University. (K 42Bb)*

been attributed to him.[38] If this is true, the third portfolio cover constitutes the only known evidence of Klee's activities as form master in the bookbindery.

There were other occasions for the masters and students of the Bauhaus to engage in common graphic projects. A series of lithographic postcards was created to publicize announcements of the 1923 Bauhaus exhibition. Held at the school from August 15 to September 30, this event made Bauhaus achievements accessible to the
Il. 111 public for the first time. If Klee's postcard *The Sublime Aspect* symbolizes the maxim that "the final aim of all creative activities is building" then his second postcard, *The Cheerful Aspect,* suggests the splendid Bauhaus parties: "Encouragement of friendly rapport between masters and students outside of work, theatre, lectures, poetry, music and costume parties. Creation of a cheerful ceremonial prospectus by these occasions." All of this had already been announced in the Bauhaus program of 1919.[39] Each year, the Bauhäusler began their midsummer festival with a lantern party, which included a nocturnal procession of fantastic Chinese lanterns through Weimar. In autumn there was a kite festival celebration where students flew kites of their own construction. These occasions were usually announced by the masters and students with lithographic cards and Klee drew an invitation to the lantern festival of June 21, 1922.[40]

With the removal of the Bauhaus to Dessau in 1925 the question of the artist's place in industry and technology became an important issue. The printing of fine prints was henceforth abandoned and instead of the printing workshop, a small press for letterpress and advertising graphics was installed. Typography and printing technique constituted the educational concerns of the new advertising workshop. Among the most important collective projects executed in Dessau was the series of Bauhaus Books of which fourteen volumes appeared between 1925 and 1931. The typographical composition lay, with few exceptions, in the hands of Laszlo Moholy-Nagy. The book jackets were designed by various artists such as Moholy-Nagy, Schlemmer, Theo van Doesburg, and Herbert Bayer.

Paul Klee drew the diagrams and the examples of form free-hand for his *Pedagogical Sketchbook,* which appeared in 1925 as the second volume of the series.[41] The typeface and layout were, however, conceived by Moholy-Nagy. His typographical work, which was committed to the *"Neue Sachlichkeit"* (New Objectivity) contrasts strongly with the expressive manner of Klee's drawings; one is tempted to see in this opposition a reflection of the position of the older masters such as Klee, Kandinsky, Feininger, and Schlemmer in the new technological and rationalistic climate of the Dessau Bauhaus.

In Dessau, Paul Klee's graphic activities were suspended for several years. From 1928 on, his print-making was sporadic and devoted exclusively to etching, unlike the Weimar period, when he favoured lithography. An analogous change of technique occurred as well in Kandinsky's prints.

The parallel approach of the two colleagues seems to explain, better than the mere absence of a fine press at the Dessau Bauhaus, why works in metal were henceforth

St. George, *1912. Lithograph, 53 × 157 mm. Collection of Offentlich Kunstsammlung Basel, Kupfestichkabinett. (K 46)*

preferred to those in stone. In 1924, the merchant Otto Ralfs from Braunschweig (1892-1955) founded the Klee Society, a circle of the artist's friends who committed themselves to a yearly subscription for one or two prints by Klee, thus guaranteeing the artist additional income. The following year, Ralfs also established a Kandinsky Society. In 1925, both masters executed a lithograph as the annual gift to the
Il. 97 members of their associations, Klee producing *The Singer of the Comic Opera,*[42] which possibly was still printed in the Bauhaus Press in Weimar, then colored by hand. The extremely limited editions, six copies of Klee's print, and ten of Kandinsky's, together with the application of watercolor by hand and the personalized dedication of each print to its recipient, clearly indicate the artists' desire to produce prints of which every impression, to a certain degree, would be unique.

To achieve even more economically this notion of the exclusive print, both friends applied the concept, expressed in Kandinsky's Bauhaus book of 1926, of the "aristocratic nature" of etching, which produces "only a small number of first-rate pulls which, moreover, turn out differently each time, so that every print is unique."[43] The following annual gifts for their society members were etchings printed in editions of
Il. 99 only ten. Klee designated two prints, *Altitude* and *Juggler in April,* for the Klee Society at Christmas, 1928 and 1929; and Kandinsky created four dry-point etchings in Dessau for his subscribers.[44]

But this does not exhaust the parallels between the graphic works of Klee and Kandinsky,[45] as some other dates must be added; in 1929 Will Grohmann's first book devoted to Klee appeared in Paris as an edition of *Cahiers d'Art,* and Klee's etching *Never Ending* accompanied the deluxe edition. A year later Grohmann brought out his Kandinsky monograph in the same series, *Les grands peintres d'aujourd'hui,* and once again a dry-point etching by the artist accompanied the deluxe edition of the publication.[46] In 1932, Klee and Kandinsky joined other artists for the publication of a print portfolio, the proceeds of which were intended for the support of Christian Zervos, whose publication of *Cahiers d'Art* had brought him to financial difficulties.[47]
Il. 125 Klee's graphic oeuvre ended with his contribution of the etching *Why Does He Run?*.

The fact that commissions for three of Klee's last prints came from France[48]—
Il. 123 *L'homme approximatif* for Tristan Tzara, in addition to *Never Ending* and *Why Does He Run?*—demonstrates the steady growth of his artistic influence far beyond the borders of Germany, and even Europe. At the beginning of the thirties, Klee was at the height of the critical acclaim that he would receive in his lifetime. His work was presented in comprehensive exhibitions not only in many cities in Germany, but also repeatedly in Paris, London and New York. The Parisian art dealer D.H. Kahnweiler became his last agent, after the sinister "great silence between me and Germany"[49] had followed his emigration to Switzerland in December, 1933.

To determine Paul Klee's relationship to the graphic arts and to establish the importance of his printmaking in the context of the twenty years under consideration, it is necessary to indicate the particularities of his work with prints. It is only a slight exaggeration for one to say that for Klee printmaking was synonymous with reproduction.

Garden of Passion, *1913. Etching on zinc, 95 × 142 mm. (plate). Collection of Professor Carl Djerassi, Stanford University. (K 56c)*

His graphic works are hardly ever autonomous or conceived from the start for a particular print technique. Klee did not experience the immediate unfolding of an idea on stone or plate, as characterized by the printmaking of an artist like Picasso. Klee's prints are transpositions of forms and images already existing in other media such as drawings, watercolor or oil painting, and the graphic formulations often follow their counterparts in these media only after several years. The suggestion that Klee's approach towards printmaking was not spontaneous expression might also be supported by his repeated attempt to negate the "democratic nature" of lithography by subsequently hand-coloring impressions and thus "raising the value" of the printed work.

Paul Klee managed his ideas like a bookkeeper. The smallest scribblings were not too insignificant to him to keep. On the contrary, the immediacy of these fragments must have held a particular attraction for him. Otherwise it is difficult to understand why he often considered these rather insignificant results for further reworking. Two examples may explain this. From columns of numbers jotted down during his service in 1917-1918 at the accounting office of the Fifth Flying School in Gersfhofen, Klee's lively fantasy generated *Numbertrees,* 1918/198; and around similar numerical calculations and elementary letters, Klee constructed his *Inscription,* 1918/207, a fragile castle in the air. Both sketches became well known later as lithographs.
Il. 85 *Number-Tree Landscape* was included in the 1919 *Münchner Blätter für Dichtung und*
Il. 111 *Graphik. Inscription* was the preliminary model for Klee's postcard, *The Sublime Aspect,* which announced the big Bauhaus Exhibition held during the late summer of 1923. (Klee's second postcard for the Bauhaus Exhibition, *The Cheerful Aspect,* was based on the contemporaneous pen and ink drawing, *Row of Masks,* 1923/254.) From the pen and ink drawing *Inscription,* the artist had already derived a 1918 watercolor entitled *Script-Architectural.*[50] The watercolored oil-transfer drawing *Memorial Tablet, 1918/8* which Klee dedicated to Walter Gropius on October 16, 1923, also refers back to the *Inscription* drawing from Gersthofen. In Klee's own oeuvre catalogue, this work is listed as number 42, only five places before the lithographic version. Klee's closer adherence to the preliminary drawing is clear here in the retention of the lower lines of the construction, the crowning cupola, and the dark hatching of the negative forms of the background, all elements which were abandoned in the postcard version.

One of the most repeated motifs in Klee's oeuvre occurs in the five different ver-
Il. 97 sions of *The Singer of the Comic Opera.* The point of departure is the drawing *Fiordiligi.* This work is dated 1922, but was nonetheless classified in the work catalogue with 1923, after it served as a model for two colored prints: the watercolored oil transfer drawing *The Singer L. as Fiordiligi,* 1923/39, and the brush drawing *Female Singer of the Comic Opera,* 1923/118. In the latter, the lines depart slightly from the original contours, as, for example, in the parting of the curly hair and in the eyebrows. In both versions the relation of the figure to the ground is almost identical. In *The Singer L. as Fiordiligi,* however, it is defined differently;[51] the figure appears on a significantly larger picture surface which, like the *Memorial Tablet,* changes the character of the unvaried motif, increasing its transparency and making it appear suspended. In the lithograph *The Singer of the Comic Opera,* which Klee executed in

Small World, *1914. Etching on zinc, 145 × 96 mm. (plate). Collection of Professor Carl Djerassi, Stanford University. (K 61 Bb)*

1925 after a drawing of 1922, he anchors the singer to the lower part of the image by elongating the coattails. The two-pointed hat has been newly decorated with bold plumage. The vertical shape of these earlier versions gave way to a horizontal format two years later as the artist painted the fifth variation, the panel designated as 1927/10. The figure of *Fiordiligi* was therefore sustained in Klee's repertory for a period of over five years.[52]

Il. 123 For the etching for the deluxe edition of Tristian Tzara's *L'homme approximatif* of 1931, the artist adopted a model which seemed predestined for the intaglio technique. The dense hatching and cross-hatching which model and surround the curved lines of the pen and ink drawing, *Eye and Ear,* 1929/306, seem as if incised with a graver into a copper plate. In the transposition of these signs of consummate drawing into oil for the panel painting *The Listener* of 1930, this precise graphic character was preserved. The etching for *L'homme approximatif,* however, lacks the characteristic sharpness of the painting and appears lifeless in comparison.

This comparison sheds light on Klee's limitations as a printmaker; the inspiration which guided his hand as he transposed the drawing into the painting remained dormant during the relatively mechanical task of copying the work as an etching.

FOOTNOTES

1. Little Worlds: I-IV, Lithographs: V-VII, Woodcuts: IX-XII. Dry-point etchings, See Hans Konrad Roethel, *Kandinsky, Das Graphische Werk* (Cologne, 1970), nos. 164-175.

2. Woodcuts VI, VIII; Dry-point etchings IX-XII.

3. Color lithographs I-IV, Color woodcuts V, VII.

4. Wassily Kandinsky, *Punkt und Linie zu Fläche, Beitrag zur Analyse der malerischen Elemente,* Munich, 1926 (Bauhaus Book 9), sixth edition with an introduction by Max Bill (Bern: Bumpliz, 1969). The preface is dated "Weimar 1923-Dessau 1926."

5. Ibid., p. 125.

6. Ibid., p. 126.

7. Ibid., p. 50.

8. Ibid., p. 48.

9. Ibid., p. 127.

10. Ibid., p. 128.

11. The pen lithographs, *Battlefield* and *Death for the Idea* appeared in *Zeit-Echo* of the Graphik-Verlag (-Press) Munichen, 1914-1915. Six lithographs, *Three Heads, Acrobats, Number-Tree Landscape, Meditation, Insects* and *The Terrible Dream* were published in the first and only year of *Münchner Blätter für Dichtung und Graphik*. The lithograph, *Potted Plants I* of 1920 was intended for the journal *Schweizerland.* The hand-colored lithograph, *A Genius Serves a Small Breakfast,* 1920, was included in *Die Freude,* the first issue of *Blätter einer neuen Gesinnung* edited by Wilhelm Uhde. The lithograph, *Extinguished Light* was included in *Das Kestnerbuch* of 1919 and *Donkey* in the deluxe edition of the 1925 *Monatschefte für Bücherfreunde und Graphiksammler.* The etching, *Old Man Figuring* was issued in 1929 as the annual gift for 1928 to the members of the Swiss Graphic Society. For other places of publication, see below.

12. Compare this with the letter to Alfred Kubin of December 12, 1911, published in Jurgen Glaesemer, *Paul Klee,* reprinted here (see p. 74 above.)

13. For Klee's Munich period, see Hans K. Roethel, *Paul Klee in München* (Bern, 1971.)

14. The Diaries of Paul Klee (1898-1918) edited and with an introduction by Felix Klee (Berkeley, Los Angeles, London, 1964), no. 902.

15. Also Jürgen Glaesemer, p. 72 above, and for the following, especially the letter addressed to Ernst Sonderegger of January 24, 1912.

16. H. von Wedderkop, *Paul Klee* (Leipzig, 1920), in the series *Junge Kunst,* volume 13, p. 15; Leopold Zahn, *Paul Klee, Lebenwerk-Geist* (Potsdam, 1920), p. 11.

17. *Diaries,* no. 913. See also Hans Cristoph von Tavel, "Documente zum Phänomen 'Avantgarde,' Paul Klee und der Moderne Bund in der Schweiz, 1910-1912," *Jahrbuch des Schweizerischen Instituts für Kunstwissenschaft,* 1968/69 (Zurich, 1970), pp. 69-116.

18. *Diaries,* no. 1226a, August 7, 1918: "Walden wants 50 prints of an etching for the deluxe edition of his *Kunstwende.* If he pays for it, he will get *Garden of Passion.*"

19. Wilhelm Hausenstein, *Die bildende Kunst der Gegenwart* (Stuttgart, 1914) pp. 307f.

20. *Diaries,* no. 1126 a, August 7, 1918: "The lithograph for the *Sezession* is also urgent."

21. The nine other prints of this portfolio were by Feininger, Heckel, Modersohn, Otto Muller, Pechstein (2), Rohlfs (2), and Schmidt-Rottluff. *Diaries,* no. 1226 a, August 12, 1912: "Received the entire printing of *Little World* (for Westheim) to be signed. Beautiful, in some ways gorgeous, Japan paper!" August 21, 1918: "Signed the etchings for Westheim and sent them off, am expecting the money any day."

22. Contains Klee's lithograph, *Giant Plant-Louse,* 1920.

23. See note 11.

24. Following numbers of the list in Kornfeld were to be exhibited: 4, 6, 7, 8, 10, 12, 13, 14, 15, 16, 17, 18, 19, 25, 39, 46, 47, 48, 49, 51, 53, 56, 61, 63, 65, 68, 70. Klee had been associated with Hans Goltz since the opening of the latter's art gallery in 1912 (see *Diaries,* no. 914). In 1919 Klee signed an exclusive three-year contract with Goltz, which was later extended to 1925. In 1916, Goltz published the water-colored lithograph *Destruction and Hope.* In 1921 the lithograph *Queen of Hearts* was included in the deluxe edition of Goltz's art magazine *Der Ararat,* second year, no. 4.

25. See Christian Geelhaar, *Paul Klee and the Bauhaus* (New York Graphic Society, Greenwich, Conn. 1973.)

26. Hans M. Wingler, *The Bauhaus* (Weimar, Dessau, Berlin, Chicago. Translated by Wolfgang Tabs and Basil Gilbert, Cambridge 1968.) p. 39.

27. Ibid, Wingler, p. 46.

28. Leona E. Prasse, *Lyonel Feininger, A Definitive Catalogue of his Graphic Work,* The Cleveland Museum of Art (Cleveland, 1972), W. 27.

29. See the exhibition catalogue *Arbeiten aus der graphischen Druckerei des Staatlichen Bauhauses Weimar 1919-1925,* Bauhaus Archives (Darmstadt, 1963.)

30. Op. cit., Prasse, p. 257, P.E. 4b.

31. The portfolio contains the following titles: Feininger's woodcut *Gelmeroda* (Prasse W. 257); Kandinsky's colored lithograph *The Cheerful Aspect* (Roethel 177); Klee's colored lithograph *The Man in Love;* Gerhard Marcks' woodcut *Family at the Stove;* George Muche's etching *On the Table;* Laszlo Moholy-Nagy's colored lithograph *Composition;* Oscar Schlemmer's etching *Male Nude;* Lothar Schreyer's woodcut *Network of Diagonals.*

32. Heinz Peters, *Die Bauhaus-Mappen'Neue europäische Graphik' 1921-1923* (Cologne, 1957). Hans M. Wingler, *Die Mappenwerke Neue europäische Graphik* (Mainz et Berlin, 1965.)

33. Op. cit., Prasse, p. 38.

34. From the flyer which announced the series of portfolios in autumn 1921. Wingler, *Die Mappenwerke,* op. cit., p. 22 and p. 20 for the following quote.

35. Every Bauhaus master contributed two prints: Feininger, the two woodcuts *Villa at the Beach* (Prasse, W. 226) and *Walker* (Prasse, W. 113); Itten, the colored lithograph *Saying* and the lithograph *The House of the White Man;* Klee, the colored lithographs, *The Saint of the Inner Light* and *Hoffmannesque Scene;* Marcks, the woodcuts *The Cats* and *The Owl;* Muche, the etchings *Head of an Animal* and *Etching:* Schlemmer, the lithographs *Figure H2* and *Plan of Figures K1;* Shryer, the colored lithographs *Colorform 6 from the Play "Death of Children"* and *Colorform 2 from the Play "Death of Children."* The members of the faculty correspond to those of the year 1921. Kandinsky's

1922 contribution, the lithograph Roethel 162, can be found in portfolio IV; Kandinsky was only invited to teach at the Bauhaus in 1922.

36. Op. cit., Prasse, W. 319.

37. Klee had taken up the form studies in the book bindery on April 15, 1921 hoping "in time to put a little life into it. Up to now the work has been good and solid, but I have seen no trace of a new spirit." (Geelhaar, *Paul Klee und das Bauhaus,* p. 17) This project, however, met "absolutely insurmountable difficulties because Dorfner himself gave instruction far beyond the regulation of the technical, and he had, as such, very precise ideas. His notions of form were permeated by the classical tradition." (Wingler, *Das Bauhaus,* p. 315.)

38. Op. cit., Wingler, *Die Mappenwerke,* p. 23 and also p. 15 and 144. The report of the faculty meeting of October 31, 1921 records: "Klee and Feininger have not yet delivered their projects for 'original covers.' " Wingler tried to prove the attribution to KLee through a stylistic comparison with the watercolored oil-transfer drawing *Chaining (Fettering),* 1920/168, which does not, however, convince the author. The angular, broken lines of the drawing—characteristic of numerous works of the Bauhaus years—are continuous and connected, which is not the case in the cover.

In 1909 Klee had already experimented with the design of patterns for the end-papers. See *Glaesemer, Paul Klee Handzeichnungen I, Kindheit bis 1920,* Sammlungskatalogue des Berner Kunstmuseums, Paul Klee, Volume 2 (Bern, 1973), catalogue no. 368.

39. Op. cit., Wingler, *Das Bauhaus,* p. 40.

40. Kandinsky's post card for the kite festival of 1922 (Roethel 160) is not included in the catalogue of *Arbeiten aus der graphischen Druckerei des Staatlichen Bauhauses 1919-1925.*

41. Paul Klee, *Pädagogisches Skizzenbuch* (Munich, 1925.) Facsimile edited by Hans M. Wingler (Mainz-Berlin, 1965.)

42. The first yearly gift for the Kandinsky Society was Roethel 188.

43. Op. cit., Kandinsky, p. 28.

44. 1926, Roethel 189; 1928, Roethel 191; 1929, Roethel 192; 1931, Roethel 195.

45. For a discussion of "Klee and Kandinsky" see also the articles by Pierre Volboudt and Kenneth Lindsay in the exhibition catalogue, *Klee and Kandinsky, une confrontation* (Paris, Berggruen et Cie, 1959); and Beeke Sell Tower's Ph.D. Dissertation "Klee and Kandinsky In Munich and at the Bauhaus" (Brown University, 1978; Ann Arbor, Michigan; UMI Research Press, 1981.)

46. Roethel 194.

47. Kandinsky wrote on December 14, 1931 to Galka Scheyer: "To save the 'Cahiers d'Art', Zervos is assembling a portfolio, for which one has to subscribe in advance, with works by Arp, Beaudin, Laurens, Leger, Kandinsky, Klee . . . The fact that the portfolio is so cheap can be explained by the fact that we—the artists—give our prints to Zervos for nothing. However, the portfolio will only appear when there are 200 subscribers . . . Zervos has unselfishly put all of his money into the magazine, in spite of debts. He wants to continue to sacrifice all his time and energy to this project, as soon as this valley of debts is crossed (as soon as these debts are paid)." (op. cit. Roethel, *Kandinsky,* p. 457, note 21.)

48. See also Francoise Cachin-Nora, "Klee en France" in the exhibition catalogue *Paul Klee,* Musée national d'Art Moderne (Paris, 1969-1970) pp. IX-XIII.

49. Letter to Will Grohmann, May 1934, *Lieber Freund . . . Künstler schreiben an Will Grohmann* (Cologne, 1968), p. 78.

50. Measurements and present whereabouts unknown.

51. Colored illustration in Will Grohmann, *Der Maler Paul Klee* (Cologne, 1966) plate 14, and *Paul Klee, Les anées 20* (Paris, Berggruen et Cie, 1971), p. 58.

52. In the titles, the accent shifts from Fiordiligi, from Mozart's Opera buffa *Cosi fan tutte,* through the probably fictitious actress of this role, the soprano "L." (possibly Frieda Leider?), to the generic type of the female singer of the comic opera parts.

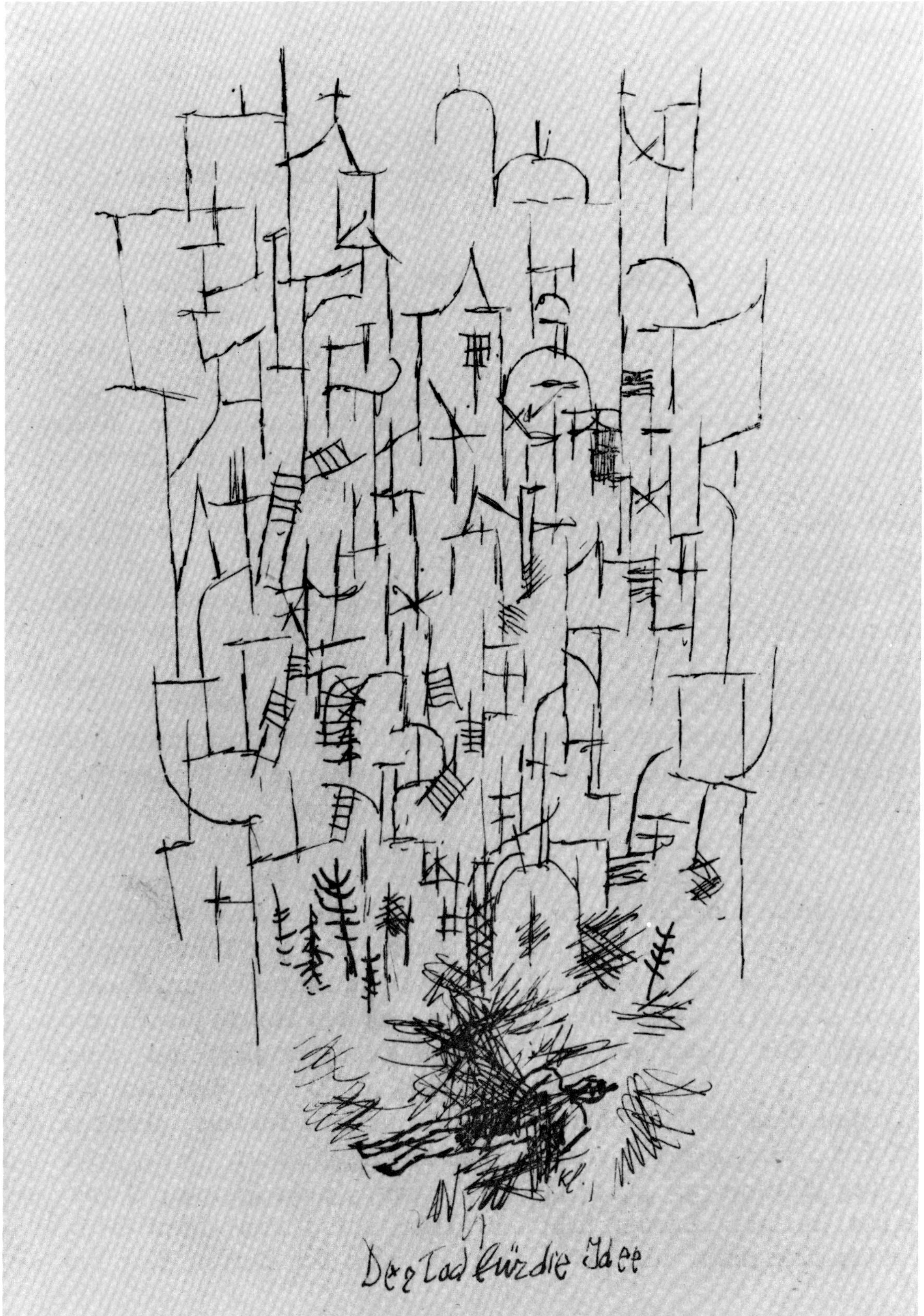

Death for an Idea, *1915. Pen lithograph, c160 × 80 mm.*
Collection of Professor Carl Djerassi, Stanford University (K 63 11b)

Fabulous Island, *1913. Pen and ink, 60 × 194 mm.*
Collection of Kunstmuseum, Bern, Switzerland. (1913.189)

Abstraction II, *1913. Etching on zinc, 74 × 85 mm.*
Collection of Kunstmuseum, Bern, Switzerland. (K 59)

Destruction and Hope, *1916. Lithograph with watercolor, 525 × 340 mm. Collection of Oeffentliche Kunstsammlung Basel, Kupferstichkabinett. (K 68Ab Coloring Type 3)*

Destruction and Hope, *1916. Lithograph with watercolor, 525 × 340 mm. Collection of the Art Institute of Chicago. (K 68 Bb-Coloring Type A)*

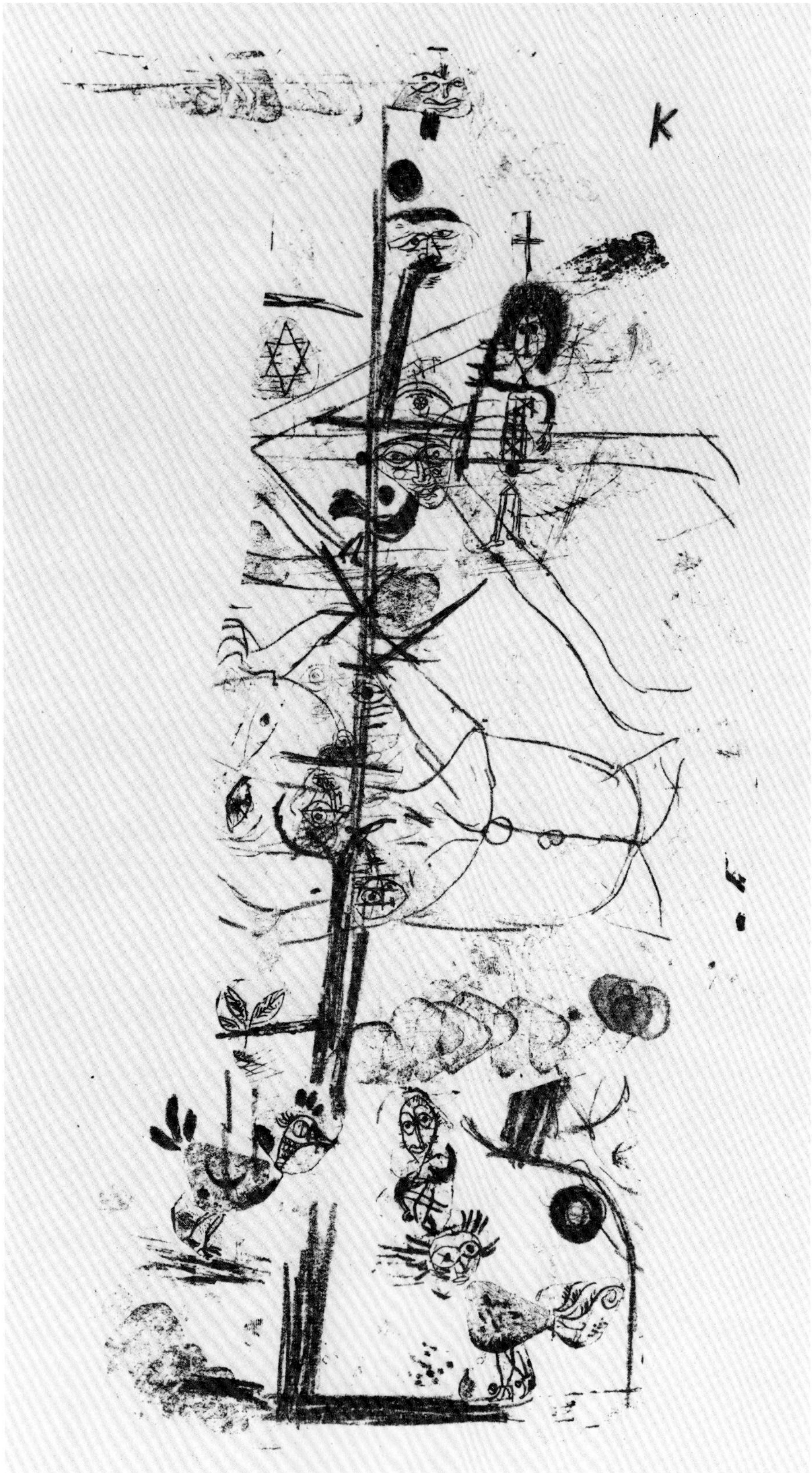

Bird Comedy, *1918. Lithograph, c. 425 × 215 mm. (compositon). Collection of Professor Carl Djerassi, Stanford University. (K 69 Bb)*

Paul Klee's Prints*

By Jurgen Glaesemer

It is difficult to choose among Klee's oil paintings, watercolors and drawings for an exhibition with pretensions of completeness; the number of works and the mutability of styles, even within a single medium, seems unlimited. But not so with the prints. Through them one can indeed make a complete survey of the stylistic development within a coherent body of work.

Eberhard W. Kornfeld's *Verzeichnis des graphischen Werkes von Paul Klee* of 1963[1] constitutes the first attempt at a complete catalogue of an entire medium-category of Klee's production. It contains 109 entries and an appendix. It also enables us to obtain for the first time an insight into the associations of form and content within a single body of work.[2] The present catalogue does not endeavor to repeat the information already published in Kornfeld's *Verzeichnis* with exemplary thoroughness and accessibility. Rather, this catalogue, in conjunction with the exhibition, attempts, with the aid of the print works and related compositions from other media, to derive new insights into Klee's method of working and artistic objectives.

Klee's prints are closely connected to his paintings and drawings. Only rarely was Klee able to develop spontaneous compositions when working directly with a printing technique. Most of his printed works were based upon at least one model, usually in the form of a preparatory drawing; from some prints he derived transpositions into other media such as glass painting, watercolor, and even oil painting. From this resulted new media categories, and when Klee reworked his lithographs in the early twenties with various hand-colorations which strongly influenced the compositions,

**Reprinted from the exhibition catalogue at the Wilhelm-Lehmbruck-Museum der Stadt Duisburg, West Germany. "Paul Klee-das graphische und plastische Werk," October 20, 1974 to January 5, 1975. Translated by Melanie Feit and Jeffrey Weiss. Reprinted with permission of the author.*

the water-color versions emerge as equal in significance to the lithographs. As in all of Klee's technical concerns, the choice of the respective printing process was closely related to stylistic demands: and therefore, the graphic work could adopt in his production different functions at different times.

Klee's first use of the etching technique dates from his student years in Munich.[3] During an excursion organized by the Knirr Art School in the summer of 1899 he met the painter and etcher Walter Ziegler in Burghausen.[4] Klee had Ziegler show him his "laboratory" and his material for a projected book on etching.[5] The impression which this meeting left on Klee can be seen in a letter which he wrote from Burghausen to his mother: "And now comes the main point: I have met here a well known etcher named Ziegler. He saw my sketch-book and immediately invited me to visit him. He wants to tell me the essentials about etching, aquatint, etc. etc . . . ."[6] However, Klee's first independent attempts at etching come only two years after the meeting with Ziegler; they were produced at the end of his student years in Munich, at a moment of impatient search for a new means of expression.[7] From this moment there
Il. 2 has survived just an *Ex libris* for his school friend Louis Michaud[8], executed in a purely linear manner without tones (cat 3), as well as the zinc-plate etching *Fantastic Fish,* one of a series of satirical fish representations.[9]

After his return from Italy, in the summer of 1903 Klee began work on his "*Inventions,*" a series of 11 etchings designed by Klee as a related group. These constitute a turning point in his artistic development, his *Opus 1*, in which he succeeded for the first time to express his personal ideas in an original form. Thematically these "*Inventions*" catalogue for the first time all of the unsolved questions with which he saw himself confronted as an artist and individual in society. He comes to terms with the constraints and misconceptions which had burdened his life until then, and he outlines his pessimistic world view of humanity in earthly bonds from which it has no escape. With sharp and severe irony Klee depicts the pathetic hypocrisy of social conventions and frustrated sexual desires; he dissected human illusions and masks as well as ugly, brittle or mutilated physical deformities. With his "*Inventions*" he succeeds in giving form to the "mire of the world of appearances," and in turning away from those depths which, for Klee, threatened to drain humanity of its flesh, blood and spirit. However, this is not the forum for a detailed discussion of the meaning of the "*Inventions.*" A fundamental evaluation of this group of work is yet to be done; but individual motifs are discussed in the following articles in this catalogue.

Klee had his "*Inventions*" printed in the Bern printing press of Max Girardet, but Klee himself etched the plates, and he accordingly jotted on one drawing, a special formula for "quick etching on copper."

The numbering of the 11 "*Inventions*" does not correspond to the chronological order of their conception. According to the *Invention* numbers Klee arranged the prints as follows:

1. Invention *Woman and Beast,* 1904/13 (Kornfeld 13)—Preliminary drawing: *Whippet-like Beast/Doll-like Lady,* Rome 1902/1 and 2—First essay in etching: *Woman and Beast,* July 1903

Il. 26 **2.** Invention *The Hero with the Wing,* 1905/38—Preliminary drawing: *The Hero with the Wing,* 1905/7

Il. 15 **3.** Invention *Virgin in a Tree,* 1903/2

Il. 17 **4.** Invention *Comedian,* 1904/14—First essay in etching: *Comedian,* 1903/3—Second essay in etching: *Comedian,* 1904/10

5. Invention *Charm (Feminine Grace),* 1904/15

Il. 19 **6.** Invention *Two Men Meet, Each Supposing the Other to be of Higher Rank,* 1903/5

7. Invention *Crown Mania (The Monarchist),* 1904/11

8. Invention *Perseus—(The Triumph of Wit over Misfortune),* 1904/12

Il. 29 **9.** Invention *Senile Phoenix,* 1905/36

Il. 31 **10.** Invention *Menacing Head,* 1905/37

11. Invention *Pessimistic Symbol of the Mountain,* 1904, July (without oeuvre number)—Preliminary drawing: *Female Nude Donning a Smock,* 1905/4. Three other etchings executed between 1903 and 1905 were not included by Klee in the series of "Inventions.": *Woman Sewing Weeds,* 1903/4; *Prophet,* 1904/4; *Lady/ Critique of the Ordinary Woman,* 1904, reworked as a drawing entitled *Critique of the Ordinary Woman,* 1905; *Portrait of a Sentimental Lady,* 1906/16, glass painting.

Apparently Klee attempted with this new arrangement to express a development within the series. However, his intention can only be surmised. It is striking that he designates as the first *Inventions* those prints which refer back to earlier models. Moreover, the new arrangement no doubt also reflects inner sequence. From a diary entry one can deduce that Klee was especially concerned with uniting the etchings in this new arrangement. In March 1906 he noted: "The etchings are now to be assembled in a single, large frame for the Sezession in Munich. Otherwise the jurors might pick the collection apart (. . .) 1. *Woman and Beast,* 2. *The Hero with the Wing,* 3. *Virgin in a Tree,* 4. *Comedian* (copper), 5. *Feminine Charm,* 6. *The Two Men,* 7. *The Monarchist,* 8. *The New Perseus,* 9. *The Senile Phoenix,* 10. *Threatening Head.*"[10] Nevertheless the *"Inventions"* etchings were never published in a continuous series as a portfolio or in a bound form. This might explain why Klee's *"Inventions"* have not yet been interpreted as a whole, although each print expressly bears the group title *Invention.*

The cyclical nature does not show itself in formal and contentual elements, because the prints are very different in format and execution. The common denominator is generated from the artist's state of mind which serves thematically as a basis for each of the compositions. With his creative activities, Klee experienced a gradual liberation from paralyzing external contraints on his work and himself. One is tempted to see in the etching cycle a process equivalent to psycho-analysis, through which the artist delves into his own consciousness; and in this context one should recognize that during this time Sigmund Freud was about to work out his analytical method for the healing of neurotic disturbances.

The three prints executed immediately after the *"Inventions"* show a formal and contentual change in Klee's style. Unlike the *"Inventions,"* which were worked to the minutest details, these works are technical exercises in which the element of chance was given conscious attention in line as well as in planar treatment in the reservage-process compositions of 1907. Instead of the symbolic content, we now have observed themes without a definite program of ideas. In the drawings created at the same time, this sudden stylistic shift is especially clear.[11]

In the following years Klee was determined to liberate his drawing style from all form and content inhibitions. He abandoned "Inventions" and thematically limited himself to models from nature which he attempted to render in a style that he himself called "impressionistic."[12] The series of variations from very similar motifs make up a distinctive branch of work. From 1910 he also included his graphic works among these experiments. In the two versions of *New Avenue* and the compositions of *Reading in Bed* we find variations on a theme. To demonstrate the intensity and inventiveness with which Klee executed these print-making exercises one must consider a series of views of Bern.[13] The view from the right bank of the Aare to the old part of Bern had already been sketched by the artist during his early school years.[14] In the
Il. 44 1909 drawing *Bern, Industrial District of the Matte, above it by the Minster Tower* he abstracted from nature by dissolving the scenery with heavy, black ink blots into a play of light islands. In a version of the same motif in 1910 a net of flowing lines executed with tempera wash replaces the spots of dark and light.

Finally, Klee transposed the painterly values of the two drawings with the aid of etching into a vibrating, pure linearity. But the model of nature still remained too intact for Klee, so he utilized an elaborately devised process to abstract the compositions further with the following "rational" means. First he traced the composition from one of the finished drawings on to a glass plate with brush and ink. "Then, I darkened the room and lit a candle, though a kerosene lamp is best, because the size of the flame can be easily regulated. I placed the glass pane at an angle between the source of light and the new sheet of paper, which lay horizontally on the table. In each case I made the most varied experiments by altering the angle of inclination of the glass plate until I hit upon the conversion of the image most satisfactory to me. But each conversion was rational somehow, by the fact that the disproportioning obeyed a rule."[15] As a result of this experiment emerged the drawing of the Matte in "vertical conception."

The "impressionistic" etchings thus were directly connected to the drawings and the glass paintings of this period. Contrary to Klee's normal procedure, the prints were for once not executed as copies of existing drawings but constituted a formal variant. He always took recourse to etching when he wanted to execute purely linear formulations of a corresponding motif.

At the beginning of 1912 Klee first tried the technique of lithography. Most of these early prints are compositions in a small format which bear the unmistakable
Il. 53 character of "studies." Only the *View on a River* distinguishes itself as a complete composition in format and execution. Klee executed this print as a contribution to the portfolio of the artists' association *Sema,* which appeared in 1912 with the Munich Delphin Press with 15 original lithographs by various artists.[16] In a letter to his friend Ernst Sonderegger, he writes about this: "I have joined the *Sema,* a society of artists under the presidency of Rohe. However, I am not in it with all my heart; my

Three Heads, *1919. Lithograph, 126 × 148 mm. Collection of The Robert Gore Rifkind Center for German Expressionistic Studies, Gift of the Robert Gore Rifkind Foundation, the Los Angeles County Museum of Arts. (K 70 111b)*

heart is more with Kandinsky, if you know who that is. I do not mean the intimate personality of Kandinsky, but the ideas which permeate this whole group."[17] With this same letter he sent to Sonderegger a copy of the *Nude*, 1912/3 and noted: . . ." For today however, I also include a small gift. Namely one of my first lithographs which I'm not sure belongs to the best of my works. Here I am again in your debt."[18]

A previously unpublished letter concerning *Sema* which Klee addressed to Alfred Kubin on December 12, 1911, strengthens the suggestion that the lithographs of this period are essentially experiments in a technique as yet untested by him. The letter will be published here in parts as an especially informative document; it reveals the development of Klee's first lithographs and reflects moreover his general relationship to printmaking in these years.

"Dear Kubin. I believe I can suppose that you do not suppose, in spite of my silence, that I was offended by your postponing the visit. I am such a bad correspondent and everything's gotten backed-up. Most people are already used to it. But from time to time I do want to hear from my friend and I'm trying heroically by reporting in this letter, intended in fact for that, although it cannot be considered so heroic because I am apparently writing to you on the instructions of the Sema. *Although the latter is still in its infancy, two beginnings have germinated, first an exhibition next spring at Thannhauser, and second a* Sema *portfolio (exhibition and portfolio are guaranteed). The portfolio of course constitutes the rather difficult part, at least to my mind. Everybody is supposed to contribute a work, namely a lithograph (signed), because a photomechanical work would not find enough buyers, and would not bring in enough money. This seems understandable and everybody has agreed. Intaglio prints (etchings, etc.) would be too expensive and would not fundamentally alleviate, for me and probably also for you, the inconvenience of working in a reproduction technique itself. If someone has already executed lithographs with success, fine, but to specially sit down and produce lithographs and to possibly give my best for propaganda purposes, that is really asking too much. That most of the members had to be told this by me, indicates their great naivete concerning printmaking. I might be oversensitive and unable to control myself, but the thought of having to do such a thing and in addition to produce something good, kills me. Fearing that you too might think the same, I would like to ask you if one could not possibly transfer one of our existing drawings on to the stone either photographically or by other mechanical means? In this I do not perchance ignore the process which employs transfer paper!*

The format of the sheets of the portfolio are 40 × 45; therefore, the image can be of any smaller size (at least 3 cm should be left for the border). Sema *is responsible for finding at least 30 people to subscribe (recently there were about 15, but several of the members were absent). I am asking you also to place a few copies! The advance subscribers get a considerable discount. The Delphin Press proposes the following: 1 ordinary edition for 25 Marks (15 original lithographs, signed!), 35 M. on the market, 1 deluxe edition about 75 M. and 15 special deluxe copies each including an original drawing (to be donated by the* Sema *artists) (Sic!) Of various members, those with the better-known names will have to be especially considered at 100 to 125 M. All these prices are not yet definitive (. . .)"*[19]

Until now, hardly another statement is known in which Klee so openly expresses his opinion on the market value of his art. What especially stands out is the statement in which he says that he does not want to give his "best for propanganda purposes." With this he not only makes a subjective value judgement of the lithography executed for the *Sema* portfolio, but expresses, it seems, his general attitude towards a certain kind of printmaking production. Also, the suggestion of settling for a drawing transferred onto stone by means of "photographically or by other mechanical means" does not speak for a profound interest.[20] Nevertheless, the *Sema* project stimulated him to undertake lithography for the first time, and to establish in this technique the basis for future projects. He executed a number of drawing experiments with the aid of lithographic transfer paper; he himself designated these prints as lithographs, although in the strictest sense they are not prints. Without doubt, he was especially fascinated in this process by the method of the technical transferability of a drawing; all along he had worked with special predilection in his drawings with different techniques of tracing, some he had invented himself.[21]

Immediately after the first lithographs Klee created a series of small woodcuts; these are the only works he attempted in this technique. Unlike lithography, the relief printing process of the woodcuts did not seem to suit him. The four woodcuts are of no artistic significance and are only interesting as experiments.

In 1904 Klee tested the relief printing technique for the first time in the zinc-plate etching *The Prophet.* To date only one proof of this composition is known, located on the reverse side of the reworked etching *Lady/Critique of the Ordinary Woman.* In his diaries Klee noted regarding that print: "*Prophet,* a zinc plate worked (etched) into a relief plate. It is an example of the style of the old woodcuts. I was able to make a few impressions of it by hand. It is not etched deeply enough for the press."[22] Klee again failed in the technique of the relief print.

Further suggestions of woodcut can be seen in drawings of 1909. Through contrasts of light and dark tones Klee achieved results by the means of drawing that strongly resemble the effect of woodcut. In three titles he even referred expressly to this relationship. However, *View out of a Window of the Parents' Apartment in Bern, intended as a Woodcut,* 1909/25[23] and *Self drawing for a Woodcut,* 1909/39 are only known as drawings and were never executed as woodcuts.

Il. 35

The Cubist etchings from 1912-1916 form a formally and technically coherent group. Klee's resumption of the etching technique can be explained by his desire for a picture worked into the finest detail. The precise technical execution and the compositional balance in the *Garden of Passion* are certainly equal in quality to the "*Invention*" etchings. 'Passions' still determine the subjects, as formerly in the "*Inventions.*" Of course, Klee's formal and contentual notions had in the meantime fundamentally changed; a comparison can clearly indicate Klee's new position. Meanwhile he had not only distanced himself from the expressive pessimism of his early works, but had adopted a new attitude which was largely to determine his subsequent life and artistic production. The passion is placed in a more universal context and becomes part

Il. 57

of a cosmic "garden"; there is no longer a question whether it can be realized or remains unsatisfied. The heroic figures of the *"Inventions"* with their consuming yearnings amidst monumental isolation have become small wriggling figures without any personal expression; they are interesting now only as formal and contentual parts within the larger whole of the Garden of Passion. Concerning the etchings with cubist motifs, see Marcel Franciscono's article, Paul Klee's *kubistische Druckgraphik*.

At the end of World War I, after Klee's return from military service, he once again started working with lithography. The following prints can be divided into those which were produced a few years before and after Klee's appointment to the Bauhaus. All of them have in common a new function: the lithographs produced before 1921 were designed and executed as contributions for journals, portfolios, or books; the prints originating from the Weimar years were created chiefly in connection with Bauhaus activities, including invitation cards for Bauhaus festivals, and contributions to Bauhaus graphic portfolios[24]. Scarcely any of these prints were conceived without a previously determined purpose. Klee's lithographs are therefore mostly commissioned works or, in his own words, art for "propaganda purposes." Klee's personal interest in this kind of contribution had essentially remained unchanged since his work in 1912 for the *Sema* portfolio.[25]

This explains why, besides the preliminary drawings which must have existed for most of these compositions, there are many hand-watercolored versions especially of the larger prints, and why Klee repeatedly took up the same motifs in other watercolors and oil-painting compositions.[26] To execute a successful composition only as a lithograph did not seem to satisfy him. On the other hand he was attracted again and again to hand-color the prints, so that there resulted a series of colored variations wherein the character of the original compositions were largely transformed. With these prints Klee broke through the limitations of printmaking; and one is tempted to classify them somewhere between lithography and watercolor.[27] During his activities at the Weimar Bauhaus he had at his disposal a printing press which could satisfy his most difficult needs. Therefore he decided on this opportunity to execute lithographs with printed color stones as well, although the mechanical application of colors ultimately remained foreign to him. During this period he did not abandon hand-coloring individual prints.[28]

For the transposition of a drawing onto stone Klee chose tracing processes which allowed an enrichment of the outline drawing by additional accidental spots and hatchings. *Bird Comedy* belongs to the first attempts of lithographic tracing in which seemingly arbitrary spots, lines and figural scribblings are superimposed and combined to form a kind of graffitto. For the transposition he used a process with transfer paper, so that the lithographs usually reproduce the drawing without reversing the direction of the image. A convincing technical interpretation of the tracing process which Klee used for lithographs remains yet to be written.[29] The drawings traced on stone are identical in their effect with the oil-transfer drawings.[30] It appears clear that Klee's discovery of the oil-transfer drawing was directly connected to his work with lithographs; this invented technique was obviously generated by the requirements of

Il. 68

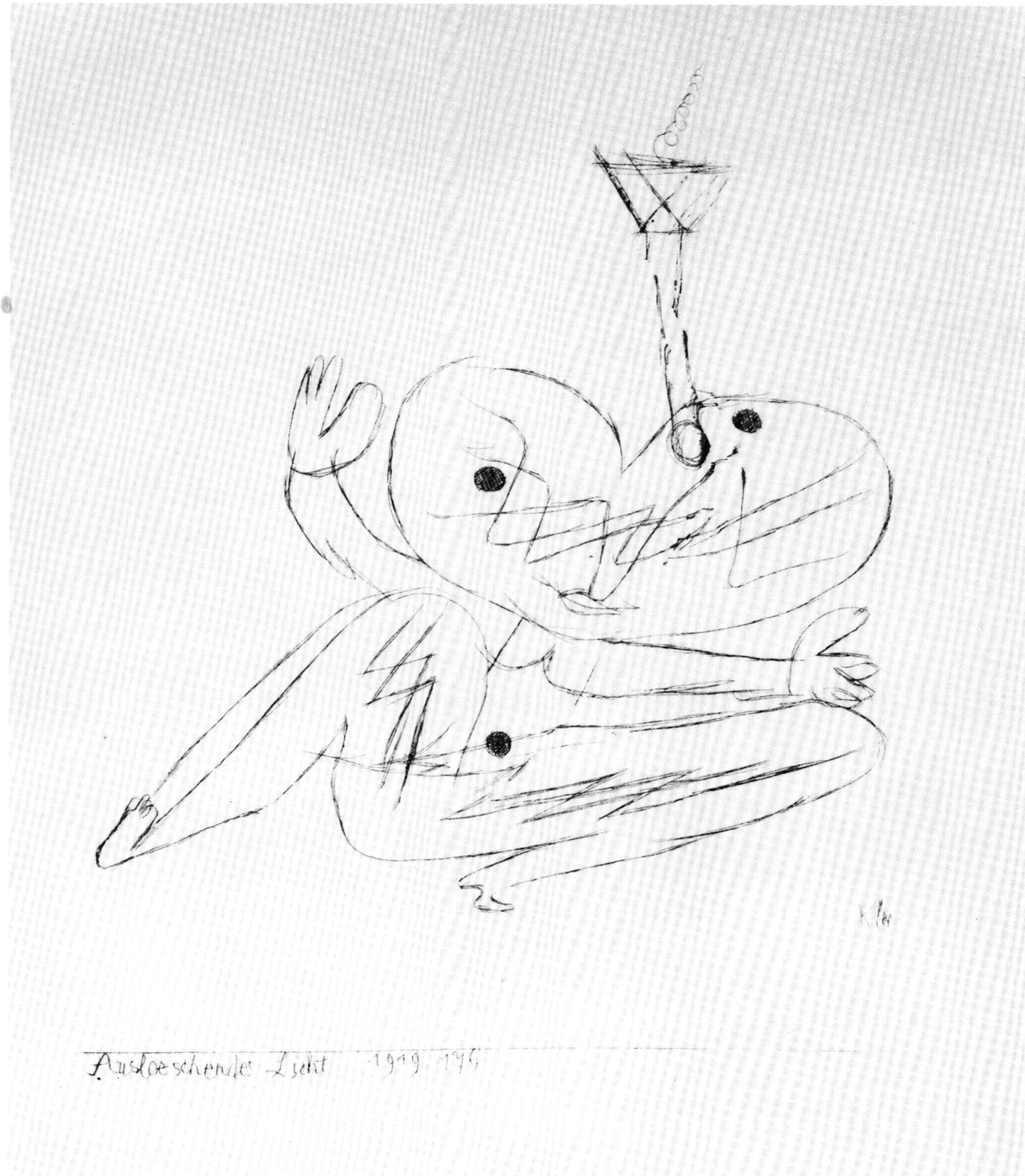

Dying Light, *1919. Lithograph, 160 × 130 mm. Collection of The Robert Gore Rifkind Center for German Expressionistic Studies, Gift of the Robert Gore Rifkind Foundation, the Los Angeles County Museum of Arts. (K 75b)*

lithography, and Klee could also subsequently use the same tracing process for his works on paper.

With the emigration of the Bauhaus from Weimar to Dessau certain conditions changed for Klee, influencing his printmaking. After an interruption of three years he resumed etching; there are no lithographs among the last prints. The reason for the change lies essentially in the fact that the printing press at the Bauhaus in Dessau no longer supplied the same dependable printer nor the same satisfying equipment. Klee apparently adapted himself to the new circumstances without any effort. In the last ten etchings he relinquished color and brought the prints into conformity with his drawing style of those years.

Like the lithographs, the etchings were largely subordinated to their functional purpose; Klee appears here again to work with the print medium only when he hoped to address a wider audience. Three etchings were executed by Klee as annual gifts for the "Klee Association" and the "Swiss Graphic Society," two prints served as supplements for the *Cahiers d'Art,* and one composition was included as an illustration in
Il. 123 an edition of Tristan Tzara's *L'homme approximatif.* These compositions were all based upon drawn sketches as well. Concerning this issue, see Christian Geelhaar, *Paul Klee's* "Graphic Small World" 1912-1932, reprinted below.

With the end of his activities at the Bauhaus, Klee came also to the conclusion of his printmaking activities. In the last years, between 1933 and his death in 1940, not a single print was produced by the artist. Several reasons can be suggested for this sud-

den abandonment of prints. Certainly it cannot be explained by the fact alone that he no longer had the Bauhaus Press, as Klee could clearly have found a trustworthy printer in Bern. Could it have been that the print medium was no longer suited to the esthetic of his late style?

In the postcard of December 5, 1934 addressed to his American art dealer Emy Scheyer he indicated clearly that the work in "graphic reproduction" (lithography and etching) basically had hardly interested him as an independent artistic technique except as a method of reproduction to create cheaply saleable works. Upon Emy Scheyer's query whether Klee could send her graphic works for her clients, he wrote her, among other things: "(The) chest is unfortunately already quite empty with the exception of examples of works I wish to keep for myself. It has been a long time since I have litho/etched. That is, of course, very nice for small change, but I do not have the appropriate attitude towards graphic reproduction, because, at the same time, I can produce many h(and) drawings or be stirred by images that wish to be born and baptised. It certainly is a (cross). . ."

Nevertheless, Klee did not completely ignore his prints in those last years before his death. In Bern he began to plan the first inventory of his graphic oeuvre, which was completed after his death by his wife, and he strove to complete his own collection of printed works as fully as possible.[31] The 90 prints from his estate today compose the heart of the collection of prints in the possession of the Paul Klee Foundation.

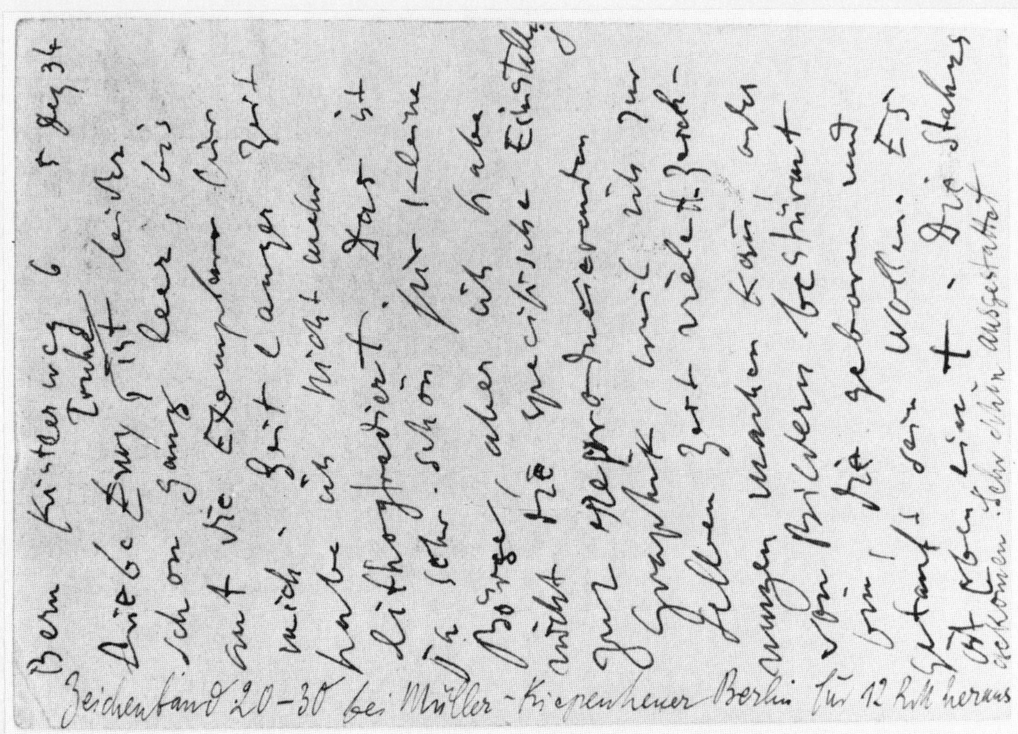

FOOTNOTES

1. Eberhard W. Kornfeld,*Verzeichnis des graphischen Werkes von Paul Klee* (Bern, 1963.)

2. The following division of the graphic work into separate stylistic groups is essentially based upon the classification which Kornfeld presented for the first time in the introduction of his *Verzeichnis,* see Kornfeld, *op. cit.,"* introduction," page 2.

3. A "Beercard" which he had designed for the graduation party of his high school class at the Bern *Litergymnasium* was executed as a line-etching (not carried out by himself) from Klee's drawing.

4. Walter Ziegler (1859-1932); see Jurgen Glaesemer, *Paul Klee, Handzeichnunge I, Kindheit bis 1920,* Sammlungskatagloge des Berner Kunstmuseums, Paul Klee, Vol. II, (Bern, 1973) p. 77.

5. The Diaries of Paul Klee, 1898-1918, edited, with an Introduction, by Felix Klee (Berkeley, University of California Press, 1964), No. 71. The book was published in conjunction with a portfolio of 25 etchings in 1901 under the title *Die Techniken des Tiefdruckes,* in the fourth edition enlarged under the title *Die manuellen graphischen Techniken,* in two volumes, (Halle, 1912).

6. Burghausen, July 17, 1988 addressed to Ida Klee. see Glaesemer, *Paul Klee, Handzeichnungen I,* p. 77, note 23.

7. Diaries, no. 152. See also Jurgen Glaesemer." *Die Plastiken von Paul Klee in Paul Klee Das graphische and plastische Werk* (Wilhelm—Lehmbruck—Museum der Stadt Duisburg, 1974), pp. 68-69.

8. Louis Michaud came to Munich as a medical student in 1901 and met again with Klee. In a letter to their mutual school-friend Hans Bloesche, Klee wrote in spring 1901 (probably during the time that he worked on the etching): "Louis is absolutely a good human being, but—stupid. One cannot say it more to the point. He amuses us, however, and we see him rather frequently." Munich, April 28, 1901, addressed to Hans Bloesche (letter previously unpublished).

9. The figure of a fish in the etching can be found in almost the same shape in a water color; a similar fish can also be seen in the *Ex Libris* for Louis Michaud behind the figure of Mephisto, on the left side.

10. Diaries, no. 764. Klee had already undertaken the numbering of the individual *Inventions* during work on the plate, which allows the inference that he wanted, with the new organization, to arrange the compositions according to their intellectual conception. It remains to be determined worker the new order also refers to the meaning of the print. The *Invention* no. 11 seems to be included incidently in the series, since Klee does not mention this print in his oeuvre catalogue.

11. See Glaesemer, *Paul Klee, Handzeichnungen I,* p. 138 and 139.

12. *Ibid.,* p. 138, note 5.

13. *Ibid.,* p. 142 and 143.

14. *Ibid.,* catalogue no. 176, Illus.

15. *Diaries,* no. 892, with an explanatory drawing.

16. Other contributors to the *Sema* portfolio were Alfred Kubin, Karl Caspar, Maria Caspar-Filser, August Fricke, Robert Genin, Frank S. Herrmann, Fritz Hofmann-Juan, Gustav Japerspacher, Max P. Oppenheimer, Edward Scharff, Egon Schiele, Adolf Schinnerer, Julius W. Schulein, Carl Schwalbach. For the *Sema* portfolio see also Christian Geelhaar's essay below, p. 50

17. Munich, January 24, 1912 addressed to Ernst Sonderegger (letter previously unpublished).

18. Munich, January 24, 1912 addressed to Ernst Sonderegger (previously unpublished).

19. Munich, December 12, 1912 addressed to Aflred Kubin (previously unpublished).

20. Klee used the process of mechanical copying of drawings for the publication of his book illustrations for Voltaire's *Candide* and for Curt Corrinth's *Potsdamer Platz* (see Glaesemer, *Paul Klee, Handzeichnungen I,* pp. 178-179 and pp. 254-255). The reproduced drawings for the *Potsdamer Platz* have been mistaken taken for lithographs (see Kornfeld, *Verzeichnis,* no. A 113).

21. Compare to this the technique of the oild transfer drawing which Klee developed in 1919, see note 32.

22. *Diaries,* no. 562. In Kornfeld the print is listed as no. 8 according to the information of the diaries.

23. Glaesemer, *Paul Klee, Handzeichnungen I,* cat. no. 373, Illus.
New note: In *Paul Klee Das graphische und plastische Werk, pp. 46 ff.*

24. See Christian Geelhaar's essay below, p. 54.

25. For this see p. 51 below as well.

26. See Geelhaar, below.

27. Of the lithographs, created before the Bauhaus period, watercolored versions of the following prints are known: *Destruction and Hope.* 1916/55 (edition colored with stencil) *Three Heads,* 1919/9 (unique colored copy), 1919/112 unique colored copy *Meditation,* 1919/113 unique colored copy *Insects,* 1919/114 (edition colored with stencil) *Potted Flowers* I, 1920/46 (unique colored copy). A *Genius Serves A Little Breakfast,* 1920/91 (edition colored by stencil, and also unique colored copies).

28. Lithographs executed with color stones from the Weimar Bauhaus years are: *The Saint of the Inner Light,* 1921/22 (also hand-colored) *Hoffmannesque Scene,* 1921/123; *The Sublime Aspect,* 1923/48; *The Lover* 1923/91; *The Tightrope Walker,* 1923/138; Hand-colored lithographs from the years at the Weimar Bauhaus: *Striding Figure,* 1923/73; *Potted Flowers II,* 1923/74; *Collapsing,* 1923/75; *The Singer of the Comic Opera,* 1925/225.

29. Felix Brunner supposes that Klee had "put a drawing on a plate completely inked up with transfer color and traced the drawing throjugh from the front side. The greasey transfer color would adhence to the drawn lines on the reverse of the drawing paper. This was then printed off onto a newly polished lithography stone." (Felix Brunner *Handbuch der Druckgraphik* [Teufen, 1962] p. 214) However, against this supposion is the fact that the drawings that served as models show no traces of color on the reverse side. Klee must have used, as with the oil-transfer drawings, another intermidiatory sheet.

30. Klee developed the technique of the oil-transfer drawing at the beginning of 1919. It consists of a tracing process, in which the artist puts a paper impregnated with oil colors as a transfer sheet between the preleminary drawing and the page (onto which the drawing is' to be traced. As the drawing was traced over with stylus, arbitary spots and textures of oil color reamined along with the outlines on the traced sheet, Christian Geedhaar, *Klee and the Bauhaus* (Cologne, 1972) p. 87-88; and Glaesemer, *Handzeichnungen I,* pp. 258-261.

31. See Kornfeld, *Verzeichnis* "Introduction," p. 4.

Acrobats and Juggler, *1916. Pen and ink, 241 × 128 mm.*
Collection of Kunstmuseum, Bern, Switzerland. (1916.66)

Acrobats, 1919. *Lithograph, c. 195 × 77 mm. (composition). Collection of Professor Carl Djerassi, Stanford University. (K 71 IIb)*

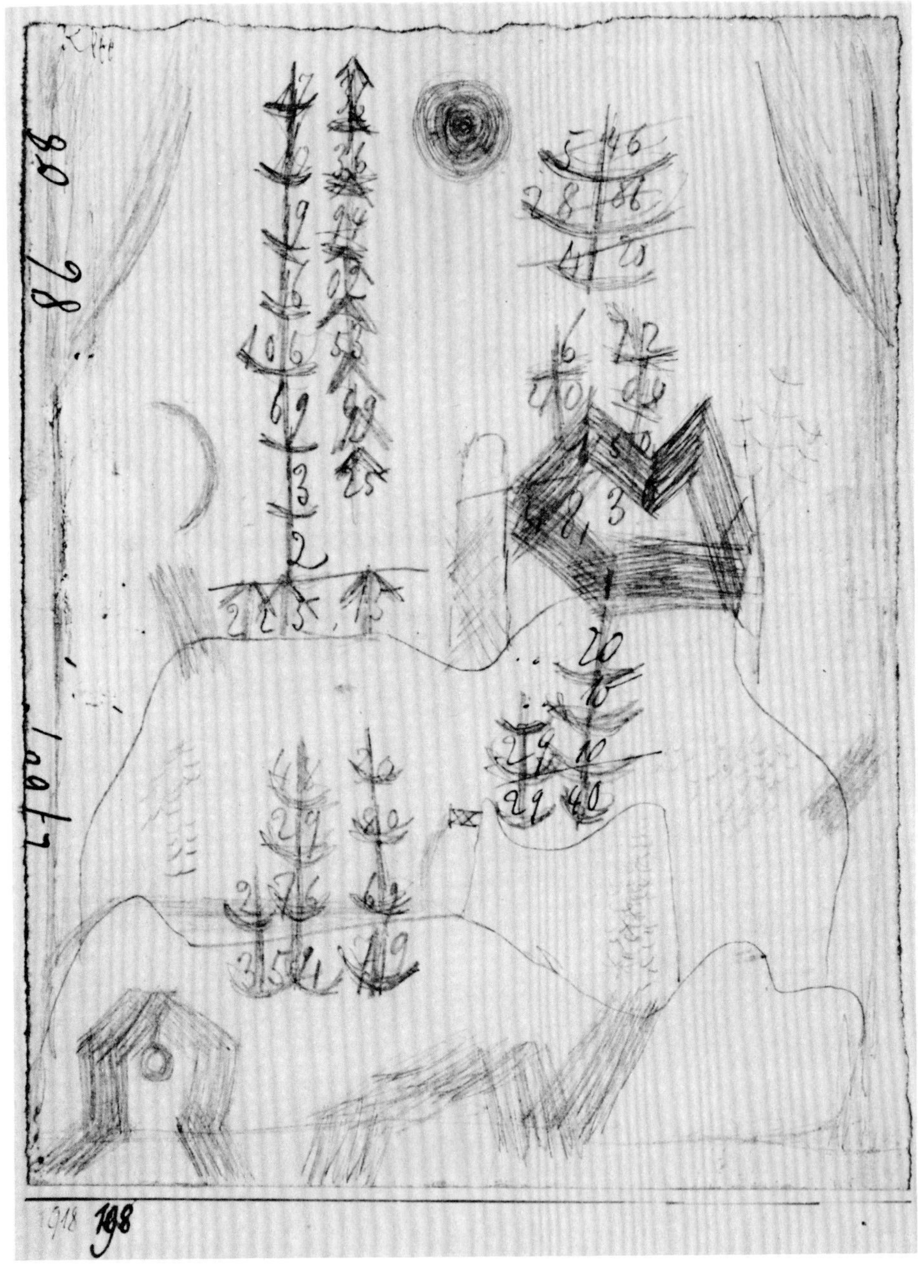

Number-Trees, *1918. Pencil, 164 × 112 mm. Collection of Kunstmuseum, Bern, Switzerland. (1918.198)*

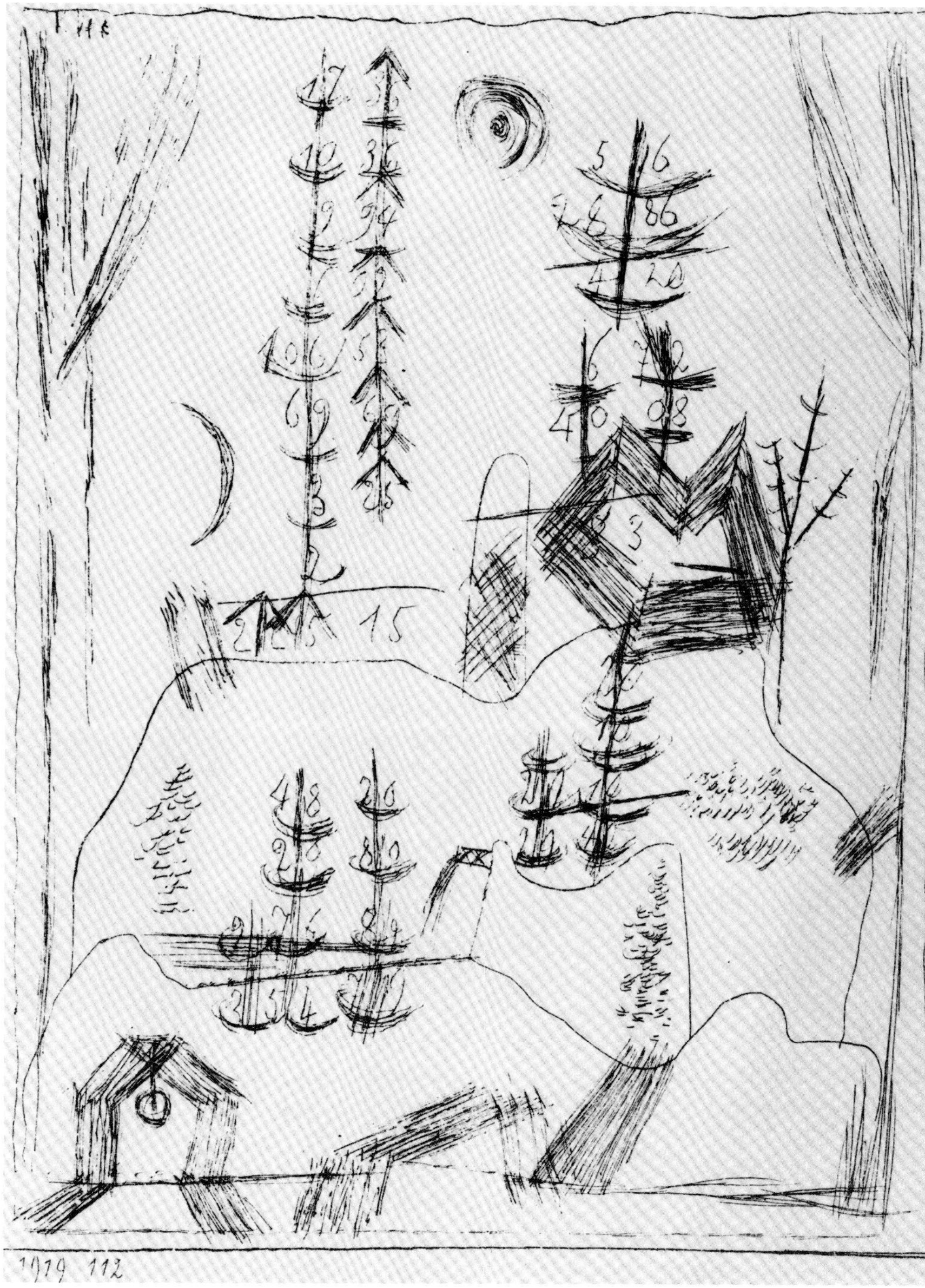

Number-Tree Landscape, *1919. Lithograph, 175 × 126 mm. Collection of The Robert Gore Rifkind Center for German Expressionist Studies, Gift of the Robert Gore Rifkind Foundation, the Los Angeles County Museum of Arts (K 72 11b)*

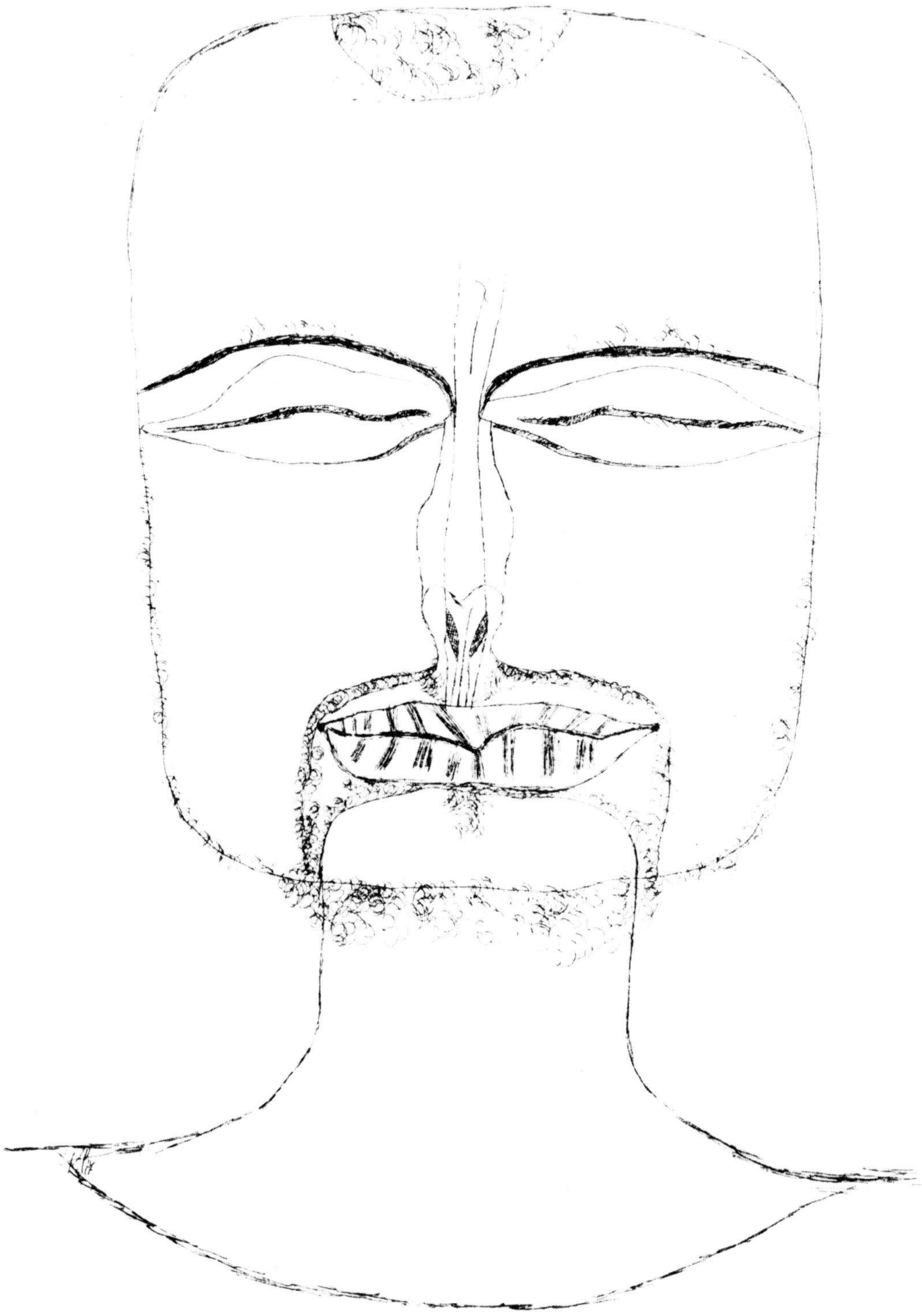

Meditation (Self-Portrait), *1919. Lithograph, 236 × 160 mm. Collection of Felix Klee, Bern, Switzerland, (K 73 Ib)*

Klee's Prints & Oil Transfer Works: Some Further Reflections

By Jim Jordan

Klee's prints became the object of renewed attention with the appearance in 1963 of Eberhard Kornfeld's indispensible catalogue of these works.[1] Since this publication, further facts about Klee's printmaking have been uncovered through the work of Jurgen Glaesemer and others.[2] The prints have figured in most exhibitions of Klee's works, but they were the special focus of an exhibition held in 1974-75 at the Wilhelm-Lehmbruck Museum in Duisburg, Germany. This occasion, the chief precedent for the current show, saw the gathering of prints and preparatory drawings (along with sculpture) for a major reappraisal of Klee's work in the medium. Among the key essays in the Duisburg catalogue were the two by Jurgen Glaesemer and Christian Geelhaar, reprinted here for the first time in translation; and significant articles by Marcel Franciscono and Mark Rosenthal.[3] In 1979 both the Stanford University Museum of Art and the Museum of Modern Art, New York, celebrated the centennial of Klee's birth with further exhibitions of prints and related materials.[4] The Museum of Modern Art's show consisted of prints, drawings, and transfer paintings from its own holdings, one of the largest of the repositories of Klee's graphics. The Stanford exhibition offered a comprehensive survey of over half of Klee's prints along with a new essay on the subject by Charles Haxthausen.[5] The same commemorative year occasioned three major Klee retrospectives in Europe: one of the early work in Munich, one of the Bauhaus years in Cologne, and one of the late years in Bern.[6] The Munich catalogue in particular contains articles which concerned the prints; and individual entries to the pieces (dating through 1921, and thus encompassing about three-quarters of Klee's prints) offer not only critiques but useful references to much of the recent literature. The Stanford catalogue, by Betsy Fryberger, compiles most of Klee's *Diary* entries about prints in a similar chronological form.

Foremost among recent writings with bearing on Klee's prints are the two volumes written by Glaesemer for the Klee Foundation, *Paul Klee Handzeichnungen I: Kindheit bis 1920* and the *Paul Klee: The Colored Works in the Kunstmuseum Bern.*[7] With exemplary thoroughness, Glaesemer has cross-referenced all of Klee's drawings and paintings that are related to the prints. Other articles have addressed Klee's prints individually, and as a category in Klee's *oeuvre.* Among specific studies, it is not surprising that Klee's "Inventions," have received the most attention. They were Klee's first major independent work, created during a difficult period about which Klee left a detailed record in his *Diaries.* A number of specific sources have been proposed for
Il. 17 these prints. Franciscono, has studied the antique prototypes of Klee's *Comedians*
Il. 26 and *The Hero with the Wing;*[8] Rosenthal has traced the influence of Goya on *Hero;*[9] and Glaesemer and I have proposed alternative sources for the etching *Dame* or *Lady.*[10] This has far from solved all of the problems in these puzzling images. Glaesemer has implied, among other things, that further meaning may lie hidden in the way Klee consciously rearranged the "Inventions" into a series.[11] Regarding the later periods, Franciscono and I have both explored the Cubist works, he with an article concentrating on a few chosen issues and motifs, myself in a book-length study of Klee's Cubist sources and adaptations.[12] In an essay on Klee and the First World War, O. K. Werckmeister has discussed the publication of Klee's two early wartime lithographs in the context of the ideological conflicts of the time.[13] There is a separate literature on the Bauhaus Press and the prints it published, and Klee's works have figured there.[14]. The late prints, usually neglected, receive their most interesting treatment in the Geelhaar article reprinted here.[15] In fact, the Glaesemer and Geelhaar essays, though written a decade ago, sum up the principal directions for the study of Klee's prints, and prompt the further retrospective thoughts I offer here.

The question has emerged repeatedly in recent years of the place of Klee's prints in his overall *oeuvre.*[16] Given the relatively small number of works and their position in the oeuvre, most authors have concluded that prints were not the major medium that drawing and watercolor were for Klee. It has been observed that Klee's first interest in prints show an overall decline through the years, from his almost total involvement with etching during the early period until his abandonment of printmaking altogether in the early 1930's. Klee's uneven interest in having editions pulled from his prints is evidence for disinterest, as is his comparatively non-experimental use of the printmaking techniques.[17] His print designs too, as has been often pointed out, were frequently taken from earlier work. Some prints were made after drawings as much as eight years old, and this demonstrates too that Klee's urgent interests usually lay with the other media.

Some interesting reasons have been proposed for this situation. It has been observed, for example, that Klee's major concentration on prints took place in Bern in the early years and at the Weimar Bauhaus, both places where Klee had access to master printers and facilities. Klee's letter to fellow artist Alfred Kubin in 1911, first published by Glaesemer,[18] reveals that at least at that time Klee felt uncomfortable with prints, specifically with lithographs, and regarded them basically as a reproduc-

Potsdamer Platz *or* The Nights of the New Messiah. Ecstatic Visions.
Curt Corrinth, 1920. (Munich, Georg Muller Verlag), 215 × 243 mm. Book contains 10 reproduced ink drawing illustrations. Collection of The Robert Gore Rifkind Center for German Expressionistic Studies, Gift of the Robert Gore Rifkind Foundation, the Los Angeles County Museum of Arts.

tive medium useful for advertisement and spreading knowledge of his work, but not on the par with the other major techniques. It may also be that he was simply not interested in the group effort required for the *SEMA* portfolio, the topic of the letter. The 1934 postcard to Emmy Galka Scheyer, published here by Glaesemer,[19] tends to support the view of prints as a minor medium, though it may also reflect a recurrent impatience on Klee's part with the collaboration and delay involved in all printmaking projects. Geelhaar has further emphasized that after the earlier period, Klee's work in prints was almost entirely occasional, prompted by a commission or a specific project that only a print would serve. For Klee's abandonment of prints Geelhaar suggests again the lack of the stimulus, during the late years, of a print-loving public.[20] Finally, Haxthausen has made the very convincing suggestion that the indirectness of the printmaking process constituted an on-going problem for Klee. A large number of Klee's paintings, he observes, are technically experimental, unorthodox combinations of various materials. Klee responded in a very direct way to accidental and momentary inspirations of the hands, and the print process, by contrast, may have been too calculated and indirect to stimulate his best response.[21]

If we must conclude, to borrow a phrase from Haxthausen, that Klee was only a "reluctant printmaker," there are still questions about the role prints play in his oeuvre. Even if we concede with the authors above that prints were not always a major medium for him, we may inquire further as to the interrelationships among Klee's several media. We may follow with interest the course of Klee's printmaking vis-á-vis his other work, and look for some additional conclusions.

To aid in this longterm comparison, we might imagine a graph of Klee's career in time, with one curve representing the main line of his development embodied in drawing and painting, and another representing his activity in prints. We may picture the main line as fluctuating in various ways as the artist passes through several stylistic and career periods such as the early Symbolist period, the Impressionist period, the onset of the Cubist period, the War years, the Bauhaus years, the sequence of later styles, and so forth.

The line representing Klee's prints relates to this curve in several ways. To start with, during the 1902-1905 period of the "Inventions," the main line coincides with the prints. For this time Klee was a printmaking specialist, in a position that he nonetheless mistrusted.[22] Subsequently, in 1906 he abandoned specialization with the conclusion of his "Opus One" ("Inventions"), and prints were never his primary medium again. During the Impressionistic period, 1906-1912, the prints still remained close to Klee's mainstream endeavor. They represented the same motifs as his other works, and they were interrelated with the drawings, glass paintings, and even with his photographic experiments with light.[23] This continued to be true during the early period of Klee's Cubist study. The Cubist-related etchings of 1913 and a group of drawings in fact share the most advanced style of the year.

While Klee's prints of 1912-1913 are relatively few, and the printing of editions very much the exception, it yet appears that he was probably more interested in contemporary prints then than at any other time in his career. His woodcuts for example

The Saint of the Inner Light, *1921. Color lithograph with three stones, in black and two shades of tan, c. 310 × 175 mm. (composition). Collection of Professor Carl Djerassi, Stanford University. (K 81 IIc)*

show a sympathy with the work of Franz Marc, and one of the 1913 etchings contains references to the paintings and prints of Kandinsky.[24] Klee studied Cubist prints by Picasso and others in the second Blue Rider Exhibition early in 1912, and probably on other occasions. These have been shown to exert a serious influence on all of Klee's work, spreading subsequently from prints and drawings to later work in all media.[25]

In 1914 however Klee's interest in prints waned as he underwent his famous "conversion" in the art of color during his trip to North Africa. Klee's central development over the next four years took place in watercolor and gouache as he produced his first major body of paintings. Klee did few prints at this time, and even though they were significant, they were not in the mainstream of his work. Only toward the end of the decade did Klee's work with prints increase again with the series of lithographs which he did for varous publications. During the course of these commissions in 1919, Klee revived his interest in transfer lithography. Experimentation associated with these prints led to the development of an oil-transfer technique which was rapidly applied to drawings and watercolors. Oil-transfer became in fact one of the leading, possibly the foremost technique for Klee's work in all media for the next four years. Based on their common conception and execution in the transfer technique, Klee's prints were extremely close to many major paintings of 1919-1923.

Klee's final ten prints done between 1928 and 1932 were etchings, although they were reminiscent in some ways of the earlier lithography. While "up to date" (as Glaesemer has observed) in style,[26] they appear incidental compared to Klee's new departure in painting of the time. Then, for reasons about which we still may only speculate, Klee made no prints during the last period, as he developed even other, more aphoristic relationships of line and color in painting.

This brief overview shows that, after the earliest years, the 1919-1923 period was the high point of interaction between Klee's prints and the rest of his work. While their number is not large, the Weimar Bauhaus prints—in particular the color lithographs—reflect Klee's most intense involvement with that medium. The oil-transfer technique associated with them, moreover, became not only the core of Klee's work in all media, but it also embodied the solution to a number of problems of form and content still outstanding from his earlier work. Even more, the transfer works express with particular clarity the theories of the artistic elements that emerged in Klee's writing of the period. A reconsideration of the transfer technique, its origins and meaning, ought therefore to shed some light on this major interaction between Klee's paintings and prints.

Over the years, the oil-transfer technique has become recognized as one of Paul Klee's hallmarks. Its characteristic line for example can be seen in the well-known watercolors *Twittering Machine* and *Battle Scene from the Comic-Opera Fantasy the Seafarer*,[27] or in the color lithograph *The Saint of the Inner Light*. The technique has been frequently described in the literature,[28] but an observant viewer might in fact well guess the process. One of Klee's purposes with the transfer technique was after all to preserve, in transparent layers, the sequence of events through which the image had been constructed. In this technique, a preparatory drawing was traced onto

Il. 91

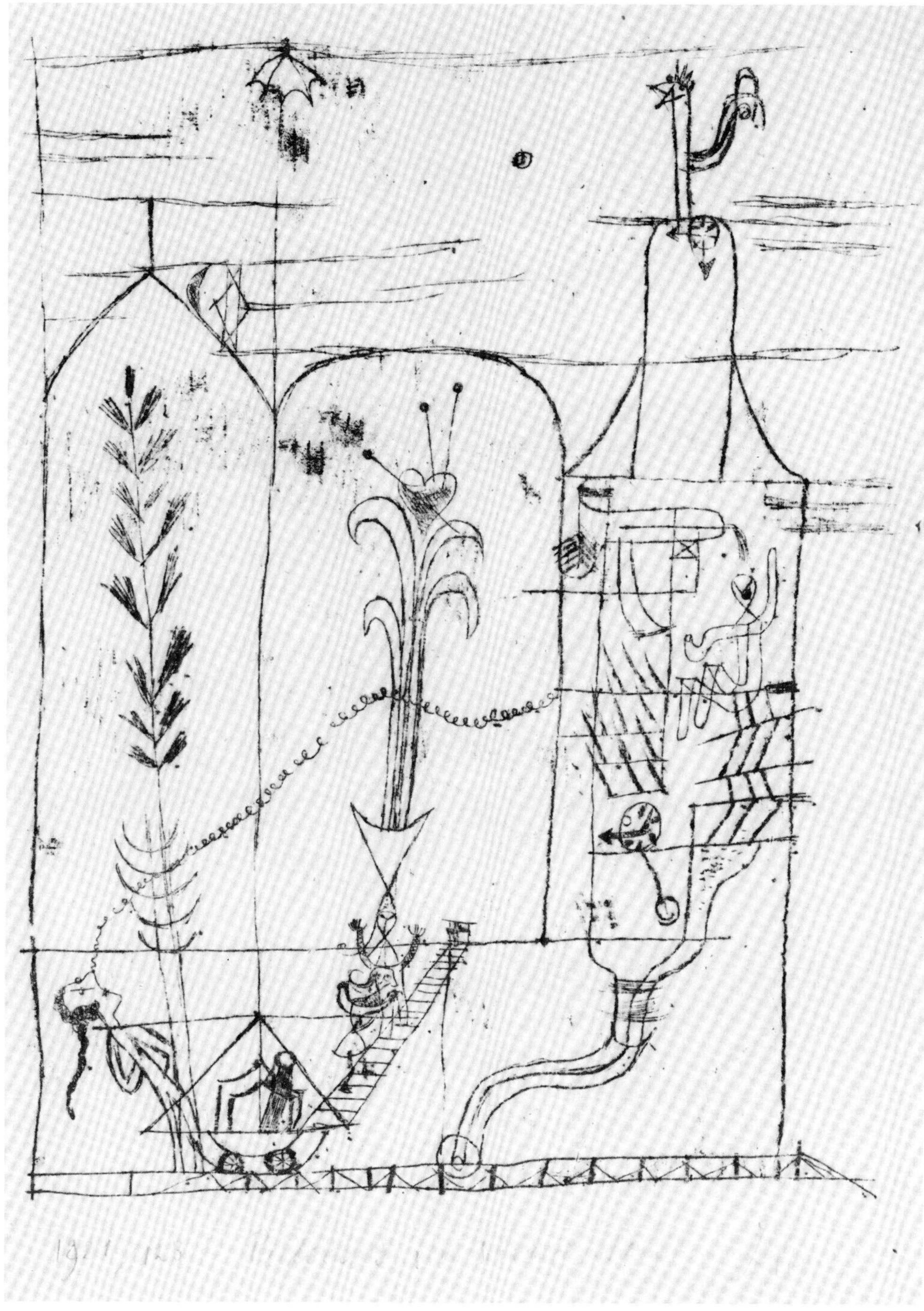

Hoffmannesque Scene, *1921. Colored lithograph, 316 × 230 mm. (plate). Collection of Kunstmuseum, Bern, Switzerland. (K 82 I)*

another sheet, intended usually for further reworking as a print or watercolor. An intermediate sheet which Klee had coated on the underside with an oily paint or ink was used as "carbon" paper. The artist traced over the original with a sharp stylus and the contours were offset in oil paint onto the paper below. The contours of the copy however were enriched by a soft fuzziness of line inherent in the tracing process, and by tones and blots, offset accidentally by the pressure of the hand.

While the transfer technique emerged, as is usually said, in 1919, we will soon see that its immediate origins are rather complex. Its prehistory, however, reaches back to Klee's earliest works. Glaesemer has outlined the evidence for this in his Klee-Foundation catalogue of drawings.[29] Beginning with his academy days, and continuing through the 1902-1905 period, Klee had frequently colored the backs of drawings with red chalk, and then scored them with a stylus for a direct transfer. Klee's sgraffito-style glass-paintings were derived from such tracings,[30] and in all probability the "Invention" etchings were begun in the same way also. The red-line tracing was laid down on the acid-resistant ground, then scratched through, and subsequently etched into the copper or zinc. With such a direct-trace process the print image was always reversed.

During the period of Klee's Impressionistic etchings (1906-1911), other methods must have been used, since none of the published preparatory drawings bears any mark of the tracing needle nor has any chalk on back.[31] The relationship here between preparatory drawing and finished print is a bit looser, suggesting the possibility that for this period Klee may have drawn on his plates in a freehand manner.

It is likely, following Klee's hint to Kubin, that he used lithographic transfer paper for all of his 1912 lithographs. While these nine prints are somewhat tentative in style, they do embody Klee's first experience with techniques that—just as much as the tracing process—would be a basis for the later oil-transfers. Transfer paper is a standard material in the lithographic shop, invented originally to alleviate the inconvenience of having to work directly on the stone.[32] The paper has a special water soluble coating, and drawings done on this convenient surface, in grease crayon or transfer ink (*Tusche*), are placed face down subsequently on the prepared stone and transferred, by pressure and a chemical action, to its surface. The reversal guarantees that the final print will have the same orientation as the drawing, another advantage of the transfer over the direct technique.

Klee took advantage of another feature of transfer paper in these early lithographs, that would also influence his later technical methods. Papers, fabric, and even other materials can be inked up with lithographic *tusche* and stamped directly onto transfer paper, leaving a clear impression of texture. Along with the drawing, this too can be offset onto the stone, to further enrich the print. The heavy textures of Klee's *St. George,* for example, have been derived from fabric. A number of drawings, which Klee did as experiments on transfer paper (but never printed) are also textured in this way.[33] While from this point Klee used transfer paper consistently for lithography, the final combination of drawing with textured tracing to form the oil-transfer technique did not occur to him for seven years.

Il. 55

Steamer for Lugano, *1922. Lithograph, c. 278 × 388 mm. (composition). Collection of Professor Carl Djerassi, Stanford University. (K 83 IIb)*

Il. 63 Most of Klee's prints of the decade, including the war-years *Death for the Idea* and
Il. 66/67 *Destruction and Hope,* and the 1919 *Number-Tree Landscape* and *Meditation (Self-Por-*
Il. 85 *trait)* are pen-lithographs, distinct from the softer, more textured grease-crayon application of the 1912 prints. *Tusche* thinned to ink consistency and applied with a drawing pen can produce a sharp line that among lithographic techniques most
Il. 68 resembles etching. The major exception to this lean technique is *Bird Comedy* of 1918. This print clearly shows the borders of the transfer sheet in the stone impression. While there may have been some initial tracing of the image from another source,[34] Klee concentrates here on the direct application of textures as he had done years before. The result has an almost shockingly informal, experimental quality.[35] A number of rounded, triangular shapes in the print probably represent direct stamping on the transfer paper with an object, such as a rubber eraser. These stamps were overdrawn in places with *tusche* to represent the bodies of comical birds and grimacing human heads. The print is dominated overall by heavy black marks of grease crayon, quite directly applied. Other traces of *tusche* and crayon may record hand smudges or prints. The boldly worked transfer paper was offset onto the stone, the only "transfer" involved in the print.

Il. 85 The preparatory drawing for *Number-Tree Landscape,* done the next year (1919), shows that Klee employed his early tracing technique, the red chalk backing and
Il. 83 stylus, to carry the design to the lithographic-transfer sheet. *Acrobats,* of the same year, has still different characteristics. Its preparatory drawing has neither the red back nor the trace of stylus lines, leaving some mystery about the manner of tracing employed. The pen and ink original was copied on the transfer paper in a much softer crayon line, and there are hints of some kind of oily tracing in the flecks and spots of transfer ink about the print, which on close inspection reveal an offset paper texture, rather than finger-prints as one might first suspect. It is possible that *Acrobats* was Klee's first print in the oil-transfer technique, but the lack of tell-tale traces on the preparatory drawing prevent our knowing this with certainty.

Klee jotted a description of his fully-developed transfer technique on the border of a drawing (*Double Portrait*) in 1920: "Oil transfer, brushed up on Japan paper! 1919."[36] The use of the hand-made "carbon" paper combined into one operation the transfer of drawing and the imprint of texture. The line of the stylus is broadened by the two thicknesses of paper. The oil paint spreads under pressure along the contours and sticks in random tonal patches. Glaesemer estimates that the first use of this technique was in two 1919 drawings, at least one of them a self portrait.[37] Shortly thereafter Klee applied oil-transfer to painting. The 1917 drawing *Evil Fate of Ships,* to name just one example, became a 1919 watercolor; and the number of drawings that were utilized in this way over the next three years is high. The Klee Foundation alone owns twenty-eight drawings used for this purpose.[38] In general, Klee was reluctant to part with his drawings.[39] There have been speculations that he regarded the transfer process as an "alchemical" trade secret,[40] and this too might explain the retention of the scored drawings in the legacy collection in the Klee Foundation.

Application of oil-transfer to a watercolor involved a special feature. The line we

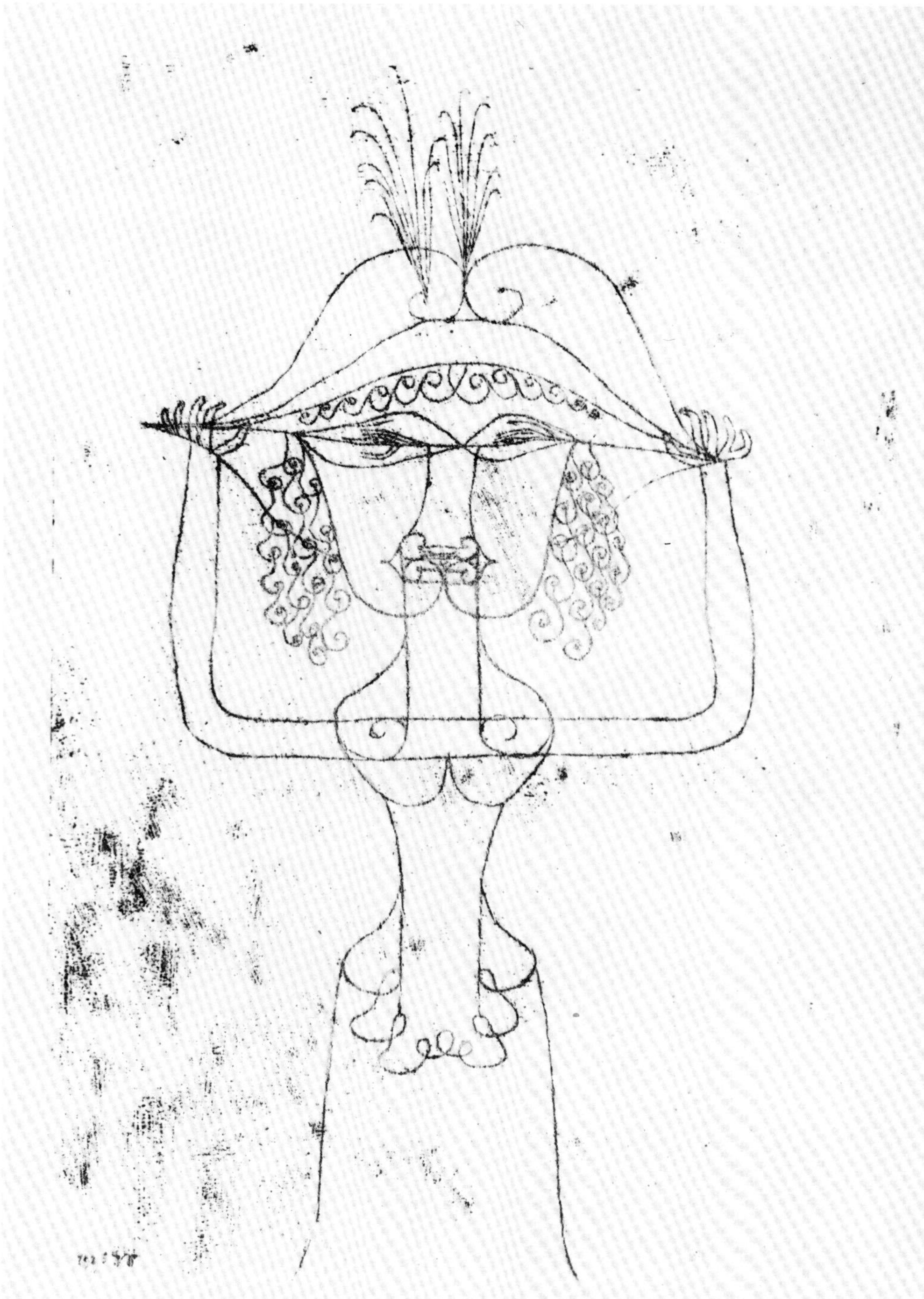

The Singer of the Comic Opera, *1925. Lithograph with watercolor spatters 412 × 283 mm. Collection of Kunstmuseum, Bern, Switzerland. (K 99a)*

see in a well-known example such as *They're Biting!,* in the Tate Gallery, was probably traced in half-dried oil paint rather than lithographic transfer ink.[41] When watercolor was applied over this, the antipathy of oil and water caused the color to recede a hair's width from the line. This created a peculiar transparency, and maintained a record of the two step, line-color physical application. Klee nonetheless continued to interweave the two layers visually, through the early twenties, with slanted planes derived from his study of Cubism, and ultimately from Cezanne's open *passage.*[42]

It is a paradox nonetheless that this technique with such deep roots in printmaking was not applied immediately to prints. It was only in 1921, after two years of use in drawing and painting, that oil-transfer appeared in lithography, in such works as *Queen of Hearts.*[43] With oil-transfer color lithography, Klee increased the layered effect even further. The 1921 *Hoffmannesque Scene* embodies Klee's fullest realization of the potential. *Il. 93* The initial transfer created the typical, soft, granular line. The "accidental" smudges in the print were not really left to chance, but were applied to the upper-third center of the design where, otherwise, a slight emptiness might have been felt. The colors were not of course directly applied, but added through the printing of two carefully-registered stones. The calculated overlapping in some places of yellow and purple colors produced a third color, a dense tannish-brown. Added to this masterly color economy are the rectangles of white reserved for the color of the paper. The visual interaction of the four physical layers produces, visually, even more strata—as the eye moves back and forth, from block to block, through Cubistic space. Just as in the watercolors, the line, bearing the narrative element, seems to lie on the surface, while the color, as the spatial element, floats beneath and around it.

While appraising the qualities of oil-transfer we still may wonder about the catalysts and reasons behind its emergence in 1919. We have, for example, examined Klee's work in the lithographs of that year, without detecting an aesthetic direction. These print commissions offered the occasion for experimentation, but they can scarcely be considered the sufficient cause behind a development which, in any event, was fulfilled initially in another medium. Duplication alone cannot have been the sole motivation either, since Klee rarely produced more than one new version after a drawing, and he subsequently turned that into a unique, hand-worked original. One key lies, I think, in the shifting value accorded to line and color in Klee's work during the transitional years. 1918-1919 saw the reemergence of line into dominance in Klee's art, a position it had not occupied since 1914. The transfer technique yielded a clearly stated line, and accommodated, as well, the rich color structure that Klee had built up in the years following the Tunisian experience. Transfer coordinated the polar elements of line and color, interweaving them but at the same time preserving their separate characters.

Until April 1914, all of Klee's work had been dominated by linear values. It was chiefly with line that he carried out his adaptations from Impressionism and Cubism. In the black and white works of 1913-14, Klee had formed a combination, almost an identity, of line and tonality. The main pattern of broken lines was given a Cubistic space through a subordinate pattern of lines, which we read as hatchings or shadings.

The Heights, *1928. Etching, 230 × 230 mm.*
Collection of Oeffentliche Kunstsammlung Basel
Kupferstichkabinett. (K 100)

Klee was frustrated with color, and for the time being could find no way to integrate it. Early in 1914 he experimented in a few works with a double-layered composition in which a line pattern floats above a nebulous, cloudy ground of color.[44] Haxthausen has ascribed these works to a momentary influence of Kandinsky's fluid color compositions.[45] But in these pre-Tunisian Klee's, such as *Genesis of Stars,* there is little coordination between the line and color layers. Klee's conversion to color in Tunisia was all-engrossing, and it caused him stylistically to completely turn the tables. Throughout a four-year period, in masterworks such as *Hammamet with the Mosque* (1914), *The Niesen* (1915), *Zoological Garden* (1918), and *With the Eagle* (1918),[46] line is subordinate to the interests of color—providing details and edging planes. The trend culminates in such oil paintings as *Composition with Windows* and *Full Moon,* both of 1919,[47] which are possibly the most painterly in Klee's oeuvre. The two elements appear almost to fight for dominance, as lines and strong colors emerge dramatically from a dark tonal ground.

In the watercolors of 1918, Klee began to experiment again with linear patterns lying close to the surface. The line is often in pen and ink of varying strength, as in *Astral Automaton.*[48] The dark pen-and-ink work over hazy watercolor in *Lamb of God That Taketh Away the Sins of the World* [49] restates in boldest terms the two-layered arrangement of early 1914. The limitation of 1914 is still present as well; the layers are separate and uncoordinated. But Klee now wanted an integrated, full-palette effect without having to subordinate one element to the other. We know that Klee usually worked in several media at once, so we can rarely pin down single works as the exact locus of transition. But it was clearly at this point in his thinking that the lithographic experiments became relevant. He devised the combination of a tracing that also imparted texture. The tonal transfer line with its hints of shaded planes actively engaged the ground, picked out the paper's texture, and interlocked visually with surrounding colors.

The transfer technique harnessed a variety of technical experiments in the service of a specific idea. The elements of art were to be autonomous, equivalent; and when they were used in a work together, they were to be coordinated rather than mingled or mixed. We have in fact observed the emergence through a series of Klee's works of what, in the realm of theory, is often called elementarism.[50] This is not the place to recapitulate the steps, recorded in the *Diaries,* through which Klee developed his theories[51] but it is important to emphasize in the present context that he reached the same conclusion in his writing on the elements, at the same time, as he did in his painting. When Klee was invited to publish an artistic "credo," his first draft, written during the summer and fall of 1918[52] dealt with the identical issues that were addressed by the oil-transfer technique.

The essay titled "On Graphic Art" is a sharp statement of the Modernistic aesthetic.[53] Klee argues that the artist must subordinate all aspects of his work to the expression of the inherent nature of its elements. He was specific, defining the pictorial elements as "dot, line, plane, and space." As the main theme of the essay he urges clarity in their use, at the expense of the traditional representational purposes:

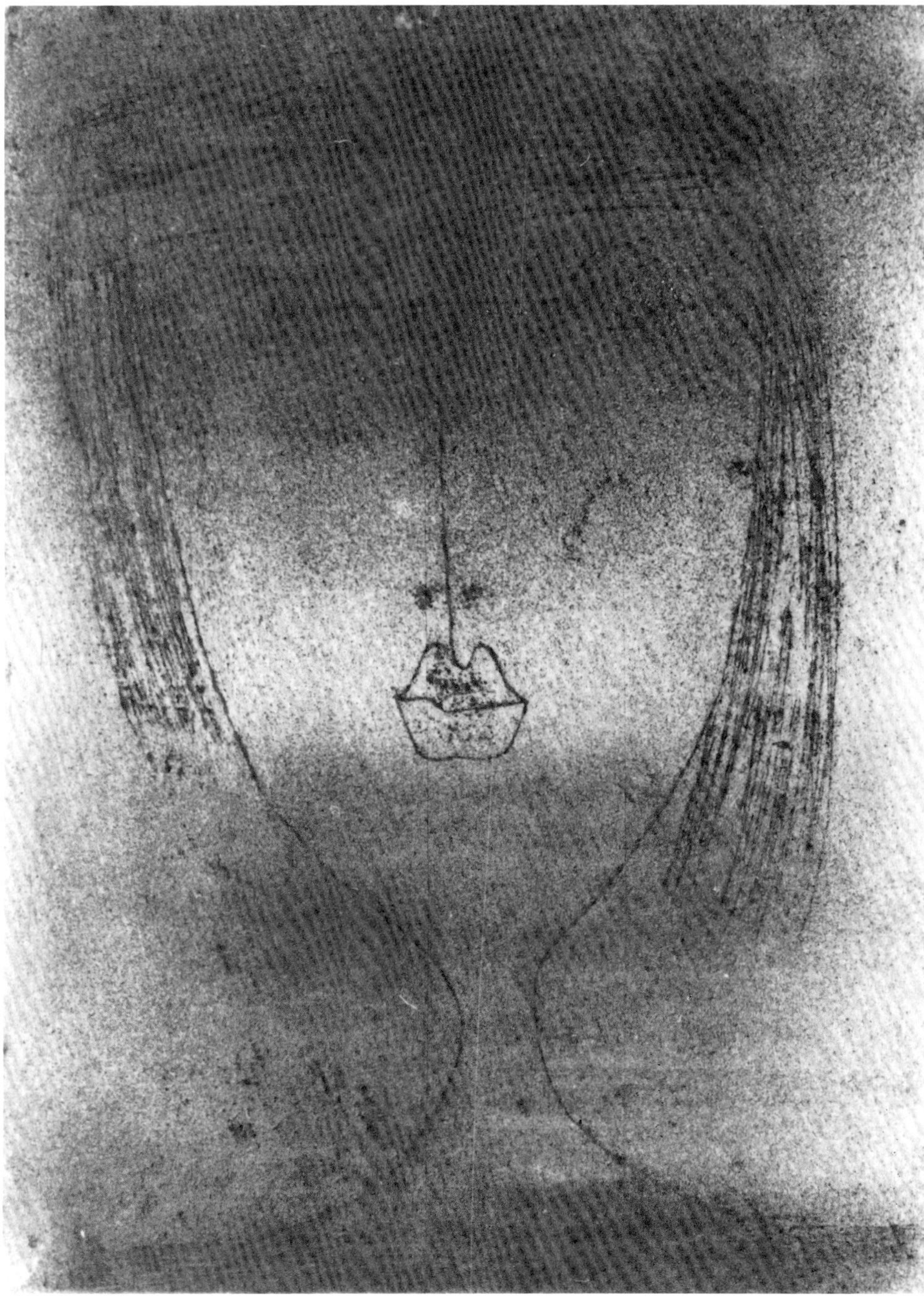

Girl's Head, *1928. Etching, 216 × 153 mm. Collection of Felix Klee, Bern, Switzerland. (K 101)*

"The more purely we work graphically, that is to say, the more we accept the elements underlying graphic art, the less equipped we are for a realistic representation of things."

Klee further specifies that care must always be taken when elements are combined to preserve the integrity of each one. As in organic things, "the parts stand in a logical proportion to the whole. Small integers underlie the proportion." The stages of construction and interrelation of parts must remain visible, self-evident. "The artist therefore should strive for a certain transparent simplicity in the construction of his work; but this simplicity must not be confounded with poverty."

Klee offers a few verbal descriptions of the kind of stratified richness that purified structure can produce. One is the image of a man in a boat. Modern man, Klee says, is aware in this situation of a number of superimposed movements: "1. His own motion. 2. The motion of the ship, which may be contrary to his. 3. The speed and direction of the current," and so forth, up to "the orbits of the stars and moons" in relation to the earth. All of these layers can be accounted for in graphic art that is true to its elements.

In 1923, on the occasion of a lecture to the *Jenaer Kunstverein,* Klee presented an expanded version of his theory of the elements.[54] The tools of the artist, nonetheless, are only slightly changed from their earlier description. The elements are "the somewhat limited formal factors such as line, light and shade, and color." The measured "small integer" concept still holds, as the "symbols" of the three elements are named respectively as the "linear scale" (ruler), "the scale of grays with its various gradations between white and black," and the "color wheel." Even in combinations the differences among elements (as, for example, between line and color) must be emphasized: "Hence, we should blur the distinctions only if there is a special and significant inner motivation. . . ." And like an article of Modernist faith, Klee declares that use finally of the "proper pictorial elements . . . tells us whether the result is a painting or something else, and what kind of painting it is to be."[55]

Klee's oil-transfer paintings and prints are paradigms of this separation and coordination of elements. Their lines and colors, just as in the theory, express different natures and yet are interlocked into an organic whole. On this central issue, from 1919 through 1923, Klee's practice and theory were in complete accord.

FOOTNOTES

1. Eberhard W. Kornfeld, *Verzeichnis des graphischen Werkes von Paul Klee* (Bern: Verlag Kornfeld und Klipstein, 1963). For ease of reference prints are often identified by their Kornfeld numbers. In his prefatory matter, Kornfeld discusses the earlier listing of Klee's prints compiled by his widow Lily Klee from the artist's notes, and subsequently completed and published by Curt Valentin as part of

James Thrall Soby, *The Prints of Paul Klee* (New York: Curt Valentin, 1945); and provides a concordance to this earlier, less complete catalogue.

2. For example, Klee's etching *Male Head with a Thin Full-beard* (Kornfeld no. 19) was unlocated at the time of Kornfeld's *Verzeichnis,* and was later published in Jürgen Glaesemer, *Paul Klee: Handzeichnungen I: Kindheit bis 1920* (Bern: Kunstmuseum Bern, 1973), illus. p. 116, d. Glaesemer also published a study and reconstruction of the reworked etching *Dame* of 1904, along with the rediscovered proof (on the reverse of *Dame*) of the relief-etching *Prophet* (Kornfeld no. 8), in ibid., no. 291; and in Glaesemer, "'Die Kritik des Normalweibes': Zu Form und Inhalt im Frühwerk von Paul Klee," in Wilhelm-Lehmbruck-Museum der Stadt Duisburg, *Paul Klee: Das graphische und plastische Werk,* Exhibition October 20, 1974—January 1, 1975, pp. 38-46, esp. 40-41 and n. 126 (an earlier version of this essay appeared in *Berner Kunstmitteilungen* [Bern], nos. 131/132 [January/February 1972], pp. 2-13). Other publications on the prints will be cited below.

3. The other essays in the Wilhelm-Lehmbruck-Museum Duisburg, *Klee graphische Werk* are Mark Rosenthal, "'Der Held mit dem Flügel': Zur Metapher des Fluges im Werk von Paul Klee," p. 30ff; Marcel Franciscono, "Paul Klees kubistische Druckgraphik," p. 46ff; and Glaesemer, "Die Plastik von Paul Klee," p. 68ff.

4. The Museum of Modern Art, New York, *Paul Klee Centennial: Prints and Transfer Drawings,* Introduction by Howardena Pindell, Exhibition January 8—April 3, 1979; Stanford University Museum of Art, *In Celebration of Paul Klee: 1879-1940: Fifty Prints* (Stanford Art Book 18), Catalogue of the Exhibition by Betsy G. Fryberger, Exhibition September 25—November 4, 1979.

5. Charles W. Haxthausen, "Klee, the Reluctant Printmaker," in Stanford Musuem, *In Celebration of Klee: Fifty Prints,* pp. 9-17.

6. Städtische Galerie im Lenbachhaus, München, *Paul Klee: Das Frühwerk: 1883-1922,* Exhibition December 12, 1979—March 2, 1980; Kunsthalle Köln, *Paul Klee: Das Werk der Jahre 1919-1933,* Exhibition April 11—June 4, 1979; and Jürgen Glaesemer, *Paul Klee: Handzeichnungen III: 1937-1940,* Kunstmusuem Bern, Exhibition June 7—September 2, 1979.

7. Glaesemer, *Handzeichnungen I,* see n. 2 above; Glaesemer, *Paul Klee: The Colored Works in the Kunstmuseum Bern* (Bern: Kunstmuseum Bern, 1979).

8. Marcel Franciscono, "Paul Klee's Italian Journey and the Classical Tradition," *Pantheon* 32, no. 1 (January-March 1974): 57-59.

9. Rosenthal, "Der Held mit dem Flügel," pp. 30-32; and Rosenthal, "The Myth of Flight in the Art of Paul Klee," *Arts* 55, no. 1 (September 1980): 92.

10. Glaesemer, "Kritik des Normalweibes," pp. 41-42; Jim M. Jordan, "Paul Klee and Cubism, 1912-1926," 2 vols. (Ph.D. dissertation, Institute of Fine Arts, New York University, 1974; Ann Arbor, Michigan: University Microfilms), pp. 24-28. A revised version of my dissertation will appear shortly as *Paul Klee and Cubism* (Princeton, N.J.: Princeton University Press, forthcoming); the material cited above appears on pp. 13-16. All future references here will be to this later book.

11. Glaesemer, "Paul Klee's Prints," p. 70 above.

12. Franciscono, "Klees kubistische Druckgraphik;" Jordan, *Paul Klee and Cubism.*

13. O. K. Werckmeister, "Klee im Ersten Weltkrieg," in Lenbachhaus, *Klee: Das Fruhwerk,* pp. 166-171.

14. As examples, Hans M. Wingler, ed., *Graphic Work from the Bauhaus* (Greenwich, Conn.: New York Graphic Society, 1969); and Wingler, *The Bauhaus* (Cambridge, Mass.: The Massachusettes Institute of Technology Press, 1969), pp. 334-353; see also Geelhaar, "Klee's Graphic Small World: 1912-1932" p. 51 and n. 52 above.

15. Geelhaar, "Klee's Graphic Small World" in this catalog.

16. See ibid.; Glaesemer, "Klee's Prints," above; and Haxthausen, "Klee Reluctant Printmaker."

17. One notes for example that neither Klee's finished woodcuts (Kornfeld nos. 50-51) nor (with the exception of *Garden of Passion,* Kornfeld 56) his successful Cubistic etchings of 1913 (Kornfeld nos. 55, 57, 58, and 59) were ever editioned. Regarding Klee's conservative approach to the printmaking media, see Haxthausen, "Klee, The Reluctant Printmaker," pp. 10-11; and Geelhaar, "Klee's Graphic Small World," p. 58 above.

18. Glaesemer, "Klee's Prints," p. 74 above.

19. Ibid., pp. 78-79 above.

20. Geelhaar, "Klee's Graphic Small World," p. 54 above.

21. Haxthausen, "Klee Reluctant Printmaker," pp. 14-15.

22. Paul Klee, *The Diaries of Paul Klee, 1898-1918,* Edited, with an Introduction, by Felix Klee (Berkeley: University of California Press, 1964), nos. 512 (June 1903) and 632 (June 1905), where both at the beginning and the end of the period of work on the "Inventions," Klee voices reservation about being a "specialist."

23. Ibid., no. 892 (1911) for a description of the use of a glass painting to produce a distorted projection, "in the sense of a photographic negative." The glass painting and the resultant drawing, both closely related to the etching *Bern* (Kornfeld no. 32), are discussed by Glaesemer," Klee's Prints," p. 72 above.

24. Jordan, *Paul Klee and Cubism,* pp. 96-99

25. Ibid., pp. 38-43, 85

26. Glaesemer, "Klee's Prints," p. 76 above.

27. Illus., among other places, in Will Grohmann, *Paul Klee* (New York: Abrams, [1955]), pp. 171 and 195, respectively.

28. For example, in Glaesemer, *Handzeichnungen I,* p. 260; and Glaesemer, "Klee's Prints," p. 78 above.

29. Glaesemer, *Handzeichnungen I,* p. 77 and n. 23, p. 116 and n.6, and p. 260 and n. 20.

30. The glass sgraffito *Nude on a Swing,* 1906.15, done after a 1904 drawing, is an example (see Glaesemer, *Klee Colored Works in Kunstmuseum Bern,* no. 12).

31. See, for example, the drawing *Houses at the Oberwiesenfeld Parade Ground near Munich* in Glaesemer, *Handzeichnungen I,* no. 399, where the related etching *Plane North of Munich* (Kornfeld no. 33) is described as having been made with the help of a pantograph.

32. For a technical description of the material and process see Garo Z. Antreasian and Clinton Adams, *The Tamarind Book of Lithography: Art and Technique* (New York: Abrams, 1971), Chapter 8.

33. Kornfeld nos. A114-A150 (appendix).

34. Rosel Golek has pointed out (in *Der Blaue Reiter im Lenbachhaus Munchen* [Munich: Prestel-Verlag, 1982], p. 308) that vestiges of an earlier composition may be seen when the print is turned ninety degrees to the right. It is conceivable that his under-image was traced.

35. Howardena Pindell has noted (in The Museum of Modern Art, New York, *Klee Centennial: Prints and Transfer Drawings,* p. 6) the artist's fingerprints among the other spots in the print.

36. Glaesemer, *Handzeichnungen I,* p. 260 and no. 668 (inscription: *"Ölpause mit/Japan gebürstet! 1919"*).

37. Ibid., p. 260.

38. Ibid., p. 260, n. 26.

39. Ibid., p. 6; and Felix Klee, *Paul Klee: His Life and Work in Documents* (New York: Braziller, 1962), pp. 204-205.

40. Christian Geelhaar, *Paul Klee and the Bauhaus* (Greenwich, Conn.: New York Graphic Society, 1973), p. 88.

41. Chemical analysis of some of the transfer colors might shed further light on the procedure. The terms Klee used for oil-transfer works vary a bit: The first two oil-transfer drawings he called "Original tracing" (*Originalpause*) (Glaesemer, *Handzeichnungen I,* p. 301; in entries nos. 646 and 647, the Kuntsmuseum amplifies the description as "Tracing with black oil paint" (*Pause mit schwarzer Ölfarbe*). Klee's usual oeuvre-catalogue designation for oil-transfer watercolor was "Oil-paint drawing and watercolor" (*Ölfarbezeichnung und Aquarell*), which the Kunstmuseum describes more fully as (in the English edit.) "watercolor over oil transfer drawing" (see, for example, Glaesemer, *Klee Colored Works in Kunstmuseum Bern,* no. 79, *Islands of the Birds).*

42. The Cubist structure of an early twenties oil-transfer painting, *Barbarian Venus,* is explored in detail in Jordan, "The Structure of Paul Klee's Art in the Twenties: From Cubism to Constructivism," *Arts* 52, no. 1 (September 1977): 154-155; a structural analysis of Klee's 1920 oil-transfer watercolor *They're Biting!* is carried out in Jordan, *Paul Klee and Cubism,* pp. 177-179 (Chapter 8). The latter parts of both the article and chapter are devoted to exploring the transformation of this Cubistic style, over the middle-twenties, into a later more absolutely-stated Constructivistic mode.

43. Kornfeld no. 80.

44. As examples, see *Genesis of the Stars,* 1914.14 (illus. in Lenbachhaus, Klee Frühwerk, no. 226), and *Villas for Sale,* 1914.22 (illus., ibid., no. 229); for the dating of these works to the early, pre-Tunisian months of 1914, see Regula Suter-Rabeer, "Der Durchbruch zur Farbe und zum abstrakten Bild," ibid., pp. 132-138.

45. Charles W. Haxthausen, "Paul Klee: the Formative Years" (Ph.D. dissertation, Columbia University, 1976; Garland Publishers, 1981) pp. 410-412, 441; also Haxthausen, "Klee's Künstlerisches Verhältnis zu Kandinsky wahrend der Münchner Jahre," in Lenbachhaus, *Klee Frühwerk,* p. 118, for the 1913 phase of this relationship.

46. Illus., respectively, in Lenbachhaus, *Klee Frühwerk,* p. 142; Glaesemer, *Klee Colored Works in Kunstmuseum Bern,* nos. 60, 65, 78.

47. Illus. in Lenbachhaus, *Klee Frühwerk,* nos. 392 and 407 respectively.

48. Illus., ibid., no. 356.

49. Illus., ibid., no. 338.

50. Klee's thought, in this aspect, belongs to a broad stream of theory among early Modernists, which is also (with a slight change in emphasis) known as "formalism." This tradition encompases Maurice Denis' famous statement from 1890 that "a picture . . . is essentially a plane surface covered with colors assembled in a certain order," as well as Mondrian's pronouncement of 1919 (contemporaneous with Klee's "Graphic Art" essay) that the "new plastic idea. . . . should find its expression in the abstraction of form and color, that is to say, in the straight line and the clearly defined primary color." (Both quotations from Herschel B. Chipp, *Theories of Modern Art* [Berkeley: University of California Press, 1970] pp. 94, 322).

51. Among the more obvious steps in a history of this development would be those of Klee's early emphasis on "rational procedures" (Klee, *Diaries,* no. 425 [June 22, 1902]) his many analyses of the elements of tonality and line (e.g., no. 632 [June 1905] and no. 842 [1908]) his concentration in 1908 on reductiveness ("Reduction! One wants to say more than nature and one makes the impossible mistake of wanting to say it with more means than she, instead of fewer." no. 834); the much-quoted passages on color from Tunisia, and Klee's continued attempts throughout the teens to analyse the differing characters of the elements of line, tone, and color (e.g., no. 928 [1914]).

52. Draft mentioned, Klee, *Diaries,* nos. 1127 (September 19, 1918) and 1131 (November 3, 1918). Klee's "Creative Credo" later appeared in Kasimir Edschmid, ed., *Schöpferosche Konfession,* Vol. XIII, *Tribüne der Kunst und Zeit* (Berlin: Erich Reiss Verlag, 1920), pp. 28-40.

53. A facsimile and new transcription of Klee's manuscript *"Graphik"* was published in association with the prints in Lehmbruch-Museum Duisburg, *Klee graphische Werk,* pp. 6-17. The following quotations are from the English translation published in Felix Klee, *Paul Klee,* pp. 151-155.

54. The following quotations are from the English translation in ibid., pp. 168-179.

55. Klee's phrase appears of course to prefigure aspects of such later statements of Modernism as Clement Greenberg's "Modernist Painting" (in *Art and Literature,* no. 4 [Spring 1965] pp. 193-201; reprinted recently in Francis Frascina and Charles Harrison, *Modern Art and Modernism: A Critical Anthology* [New York: Harper and Row, 1982] pp. 5-10).

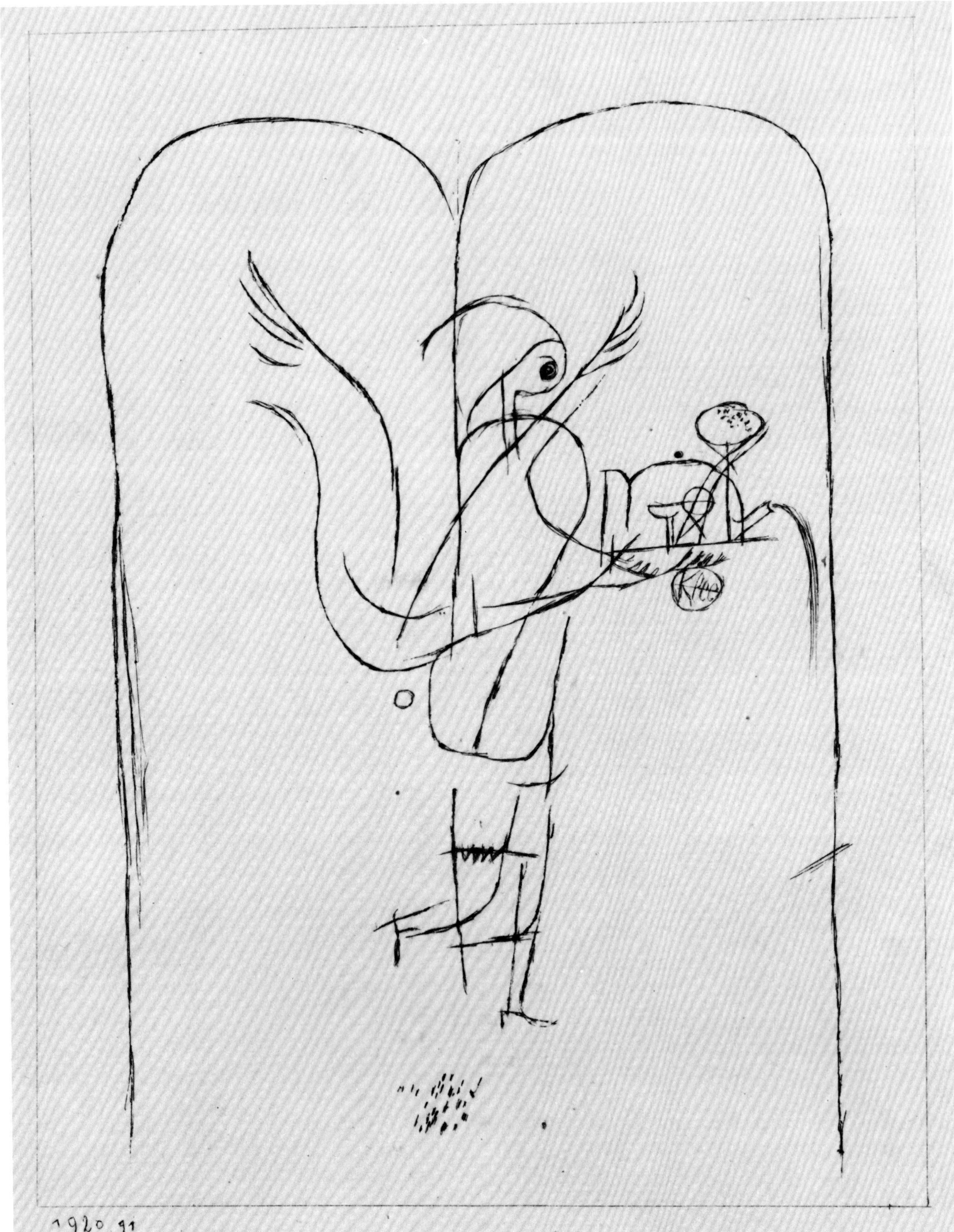

A Genius Serves a Little Breakfast, *1920. Lithograph without color,*
c. 255 × 175 mm. (composition).
Collection of Oeffentliche Kunstsammlung Basel, Kupferstickkabinett. (K 79 I)

A Genius Serves a Little Breakfast, 1920.
Lithograph with water color, c. 255 × 175. mm. (composition). Collection of Professor Carl Djerassi, Stanford University. (K 72 IIc)

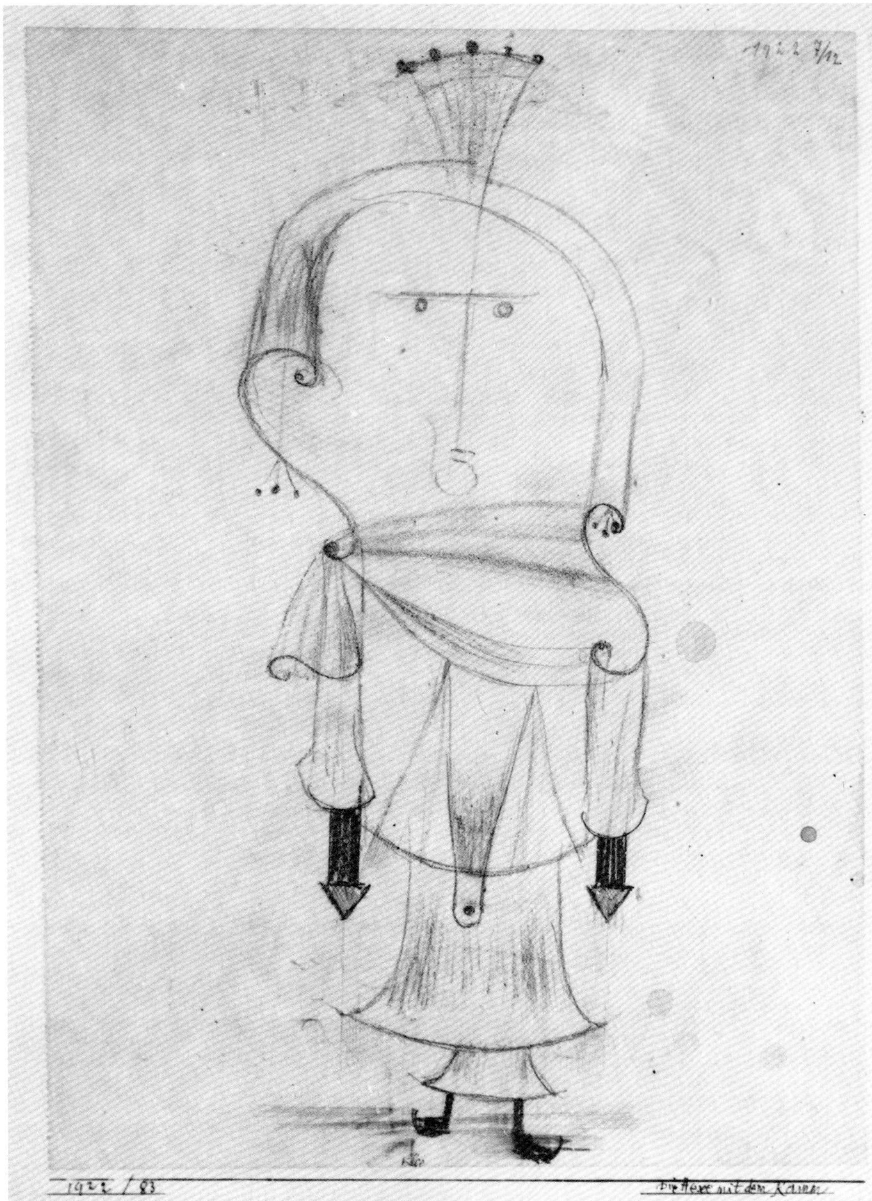

The Witch With the Comb, *1922. Pencil, 288 × 210 mm.*
Collection of Galerie Rosengart, Lucerne, Switzerland. (1922.83)

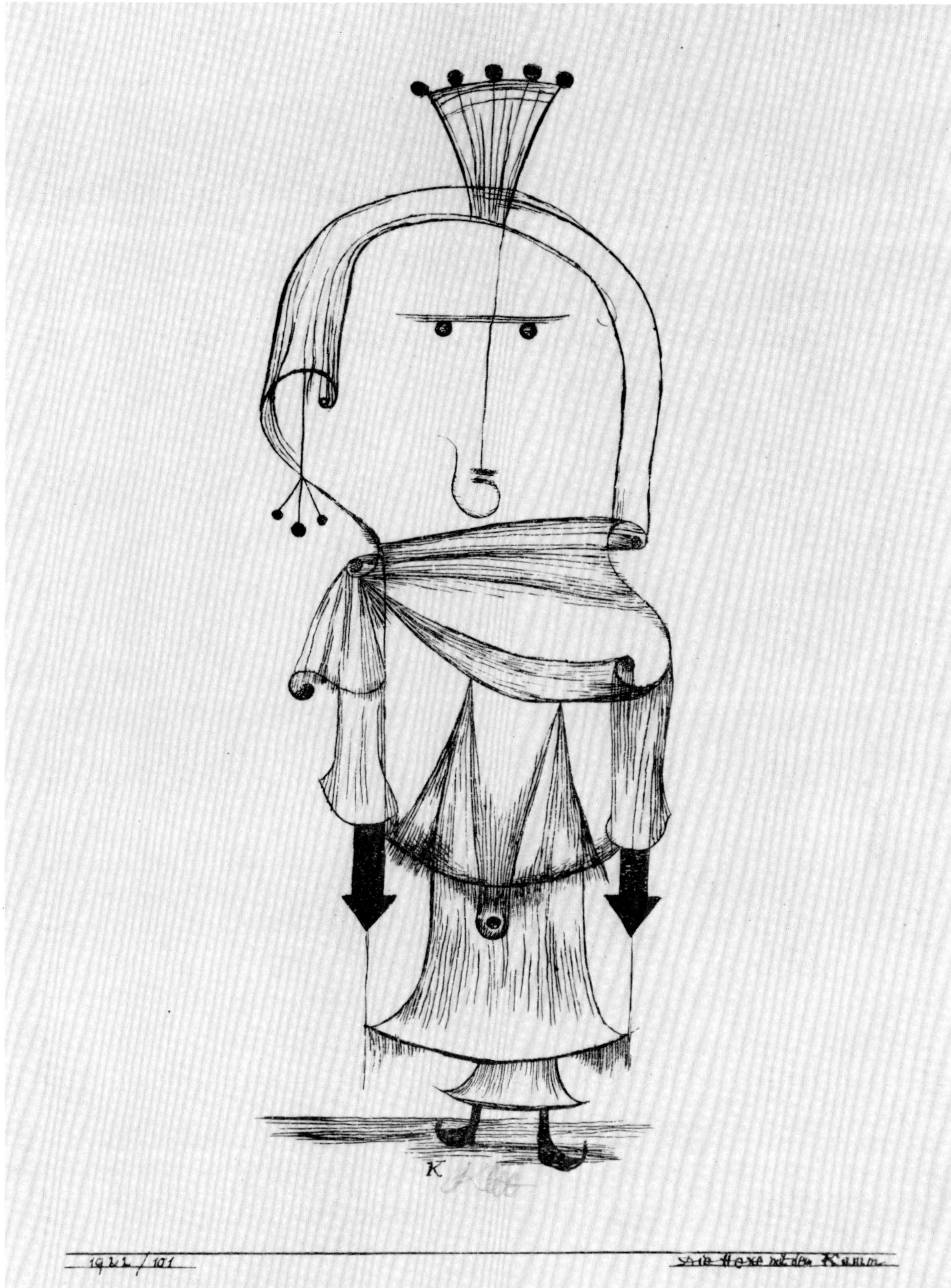

The Witch with the Comb, *1922. Lithograph, c. 310 × 210 mm. (composition)*
Collection of Professor Carl Djerassi, Stanford University. (K 86 Bb)

Inscription, *1918. Pen & ink, 210 × 750 mm. Collection of Felix Klee, Bern, Switzerland. (1918.207)*

The Loftier Aspect-*Bauhaus Postcard, 1923. Color Lithograph, c. 140 × 75 mm. (composition)*
Collection of Professor Carl Djerassi, Stanford University. (K 88 IIIb)

Man in Love, *1922, Pencil, 213 × 160 mm. Collection of Galerie Rosengart, Lucerne, Switzerland. (1922.201)*

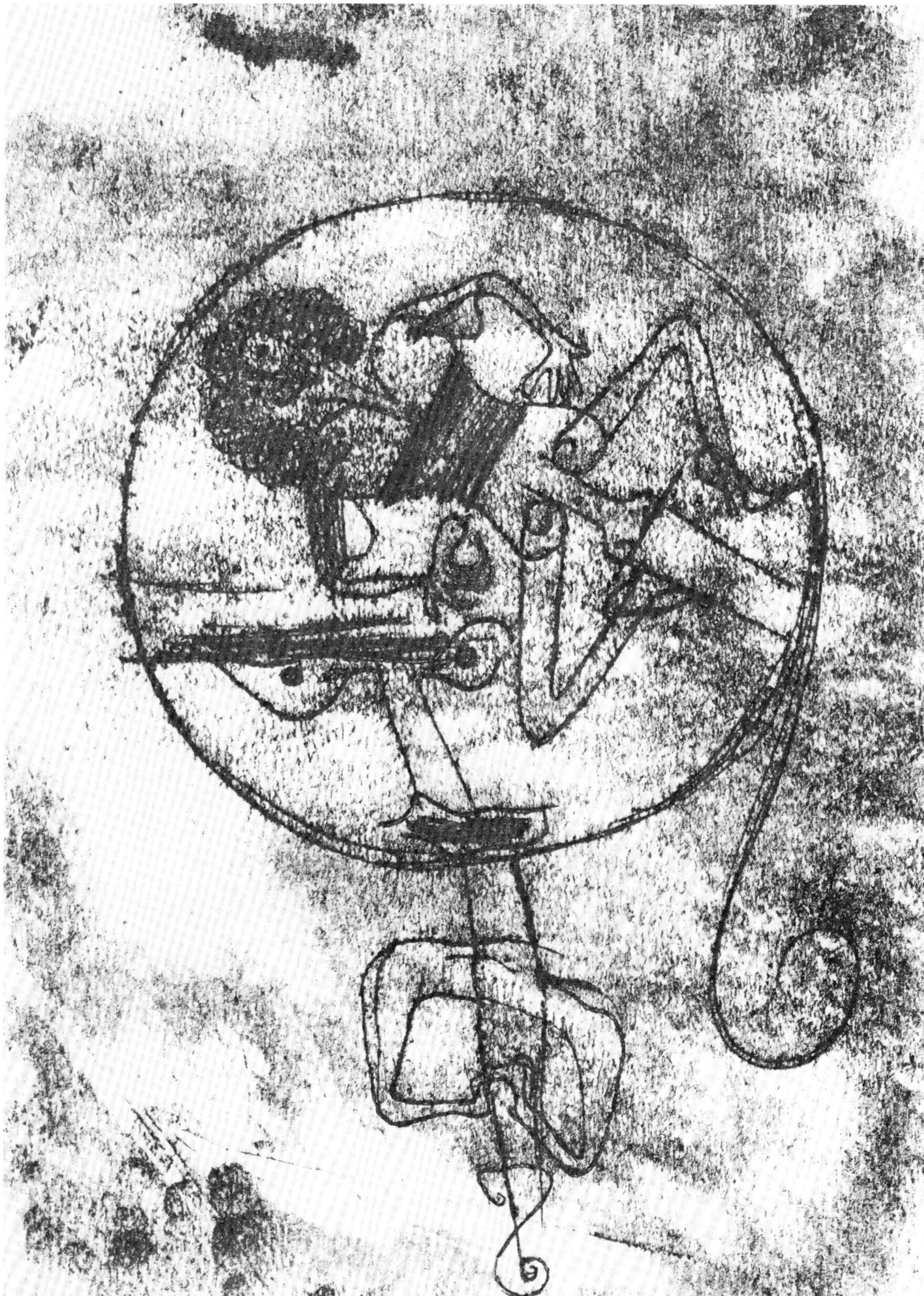

The Man in Love, *1923. Color lithograph with two stones, black and tan 275 × 190 mm. (composition). Collection of Professor Carl Djerassi, Stanford University. (K 94 IIIb)*

Exhibition Checklist

PRINTS*

1. Ex Libris L. Michaud, 1901. Etching, 158 × 116 mm. *Collection of Felix Klee, Bern, Switzerland. (K 2)*

2. Comedian, 1903. Etching on zinc, 118 × 161 mm. (ohne Facette). *Collection of Oeffentliche Kunstammlung Basel, Kupferstichkabinett. (K 6).*

3. Virgin in the Tree, 1903. Etching, 236 × 298 mm. (plate). *Courtesy of Alice Adam Ltd., Chicago, Illinois (K 4)*

4. Virgin in the Tree, 1903. Etching on zinc, 236 × 298 mm. (plate). *Collection of Professor Carl Djerassi, Stanford University. (K 4b)*

5. Two Men Meet, Each Supposing the Other of Higher Rank, 1903. *Etching on zinc, 118 ×* 225 mm. (plate). *Collection of Professor Carl Djerassi, Stanford University. (K 7IIa)*

6. The Comedian, 1904. Etching on zinc, 153 × 168 mm. (plate). *Collection of Professor Carl Djerassi, Stanford University. (K 10 IIb)*

7. Woman and Beast, 1904. Etching on zinc, 200 × 228 mm. (plate). *Collection of Professor Carl Djerassi, Stanford University. (K 13b)*

8. Man Groveling Before a Crown (Crown Mania), 1904. Etching on zinc, 160 × 160 mm. (plate). *Collection of Professor Carl Djerassi, Stanford University. (K 14b)*

9. Charm, 1904. Etching on zinc, 133 × 92 mm. (plate). *Collection of Professor Carl Djerassi, Stanford University. (K 12a)*

10. Perseus: The Triumph of Wit Over Misfortune, 1904. Etching on zinc, 128 × 143 mm. (plate). *Collection of Professor Carl Djerassi, Stanford University. (K 15a)*

11. Prophet, 1904. Relief etching on zinc, trial proof of relief etching in goauche color, 120 × 120 mm. *Collection of Kunstmuseum, Bern, Switzerland. (K 8).* Verso—**Lady: Critique of the Normal Woman,** 1904-5. Etching reworked as a pencil and ink drawing, 248 × 189 mm.

12. Pessimistic Symbol of the Mountain, 1904. Etching on zinc, 146 × 69 mm. *Collection of Kunstmuseum, Bern, Switzerland. (K 11)*

*Numbers refer to the system in the book by Eberhard W. Kornfeld, *Verzeichnis des graphischen Werkes von Paul Klee* (Bern, 1963).

13. Menacing Head, 1905. Etching on zinc, 200 × 145 mm. (plate). *Collection of Professor Carl Djerassi, Stanford University. (K 18 a)*

14. The Hero with the Wing, 1905. Etching on zinc, 257 × 160 mm. (plate). *Collection of the Art Institute of Chicago. (K 16).*

15. The Senile Phoenix, 1905. Etching on zinc, 270 × 198 mm. (plate). *Collection of Professor Carl Djerassi, Stanford University. (K 17 IIb)*

16. Suburban Villas, 1910. Etching on zinc, 113 × 228 mm. *Collection of Kunstmuseum, Bern, Switzerland. (K 27)*

17. New Avenue—First Version, 1910. Etching on zinc, 152 × 17 mm. *Collection of Felix Klee, Bern, Switzerland, (K 22)*

18. Three Girls in the Meadow, 1910. Etching on copper, 144 × 118 mm. *Collection of Kunstmuseum, Bern, Switzerland. (K 28)*

19. Sheep in the Pen, 1910. Etching on zinc, 75 × 265 mm. *Collection of Kunstmuseum, Bern, Switzerland. (K 30)*

20. Bern, 1910. Etching on zinc, 107 × 148 mm. *Collection of Kunstmuseum, Bern, Switzerland. (K 32)*

21. Plain North of Munich, 1910. Etching on zinc, 106 × 148 mm. *Collection of Kunstmuseum, Bern, Switzerland. (K 33)*

22. Garden, 1910. Drypoint, 96 × 130 mm. *Collection of The Museum of Modern Art, New York, Gift of Curt Valentin. (K 25)*

23. Railway Station, 1911. Drypoint, 148 × 198 mm. *Collection of Städitsche Galerie im Lenbachhaus, Munich, West Germany. (K 37a)*

24. Steamships in the Harbor, 1911. Drypoint etching, 148 × 197 mm. *Collection of Kunstmuseum, Bern, Switzerland. (K 38)*

25. Head of a Young Girl, *Hannah en face,* 1912. Drypoint, 118 × 74 mm. *Collection of Kunstmuseum, Bern, Switzerland. (K 45)*

26. Reclining Figure, 1912. Woodcut, 68 × 215 mm. *Collection of Kunstmuseum, Bern, Switzerland. (K 50)*

27. Fragment of a Woodcut, 1912. Woodcut, 98 × 80 mm. *Collection of Felix Klee, Bern, Switzerland. (K 52)*

28. Remorse, 1912. Woodcut, 111 × 101 mm. *Collection of Felix Klee, Bern, Switzerland. (K 49)*

29. St. George, 1912. Lithograph, 53 × 157 mm. *Collection of Offentliche Kunstsammlung Basel, Kupferstichkabinett. (K 46)*

30. View on a River, 1912. Lithograph, c.197 × 285 mm. (composition). Collection of Professor Carl Djerassi, Stanford University. (K 42 Bb)

31. Tragedy on Stilts, 1912. Lithograph, c.92 × 95 mm. (composition). *Collection of Professor Carl Djerassi, Stanford University. (K 48b)*

32. At the Window, 1912. Lithograph, 131 × 100 mm. Collection of the Djerassi Foundation. (K 53)

33. Street Urchins, 1912. Lithograph, 77 × 120 mm. *Collection of Stadtische Galerie im Lenbachhaus, Munich, West Germany. (K 47)*

34. Pomp in Miniature, 1913. Etching on zinc, 75 × 59 mm. *Collection of Kunstmuseum, Bern, Switzerland. (K 55)*

35. Abstraction II, 1913. Etching on zinc, 74 × 85 mm. *Collection of Kunstmuseum, Bern, Switzerland. (K 59)*

36. Garden of Passion, 1913. Etching on zinc, 95 × 142 mm. (plate). *Collection of Professor Carl Djerassi, Stanford University. (K 56c)*

37. Battlefield, 1914. Feder lithograph, 68 × 108 mm. *Collection of The Robert Gore Rifkind Center for German Expressionist Studies, gift of the Robert Gore Rifkind Foundation, The Los Angeles County Museum of Art. (K 62II)*

38. Small World, 1914. Etching on zinc, 145 × 96 mm. (plate). *Collection of Professor Carl Djerassi, Stanford University. (K 61 Bb)*

39. Park, 1920. Facsimile lithograph after a 1914 watercolor, 127 × 102 mm. *Collection of Professor Carl Djerassi, Stanford University. (K A112)*

40. Death for the Idea, 1915. Pen lithograph, c.160 × 80 mm. (composition) *Collection of Professor Carl Djerassi, Stanford University. (K 63IIb)*

41. Reflections in a Window, 1915. Etching, 160 × 115 mm. (plate). *Collection of Djerassi Foundation. (K 64)*

42. Little Castle in the Air, 1915. Etching on zinc, 90 × 213 mm. (plate). *Collection of Professor Carl Djerassi, Stanford University. (K 65b)*

43. Destruction and Hope, 1916. Lithograph with watercolor, 525 × 340 mm. *Collection of the Art Institute of Chicago. (K 68 Bb-Coloring Type A)*

44. Destruction and Hope, 1916. Lithograph with watercolor, 525 × 340 mm. *Collection of Oeffentliche Kunstsammlung Basel, Kupferstichkabinett. (K 68 Ab. Coloring Type 3)*

45. Bird Comedy, 1918. Lithograph, c.425 × 215 mm. (composition). *Collection of Professor Carl Djerassi, Stanford University. (K 69 Bb)*

46. Meditation (Self-Portrait), 1919. Lithograph, 236 × 160 mm. *Collection of The Robert Gore Rifkind Center for German Expressionist Studies, Gift of the Robert Gore Rifkind Foundation, The Los Angeles County Museum of Art. (K 73 IIb)*

47. Meditation (Self-Portrait), 1919. Hand colored lithograph, 236 × 160 mm. *Collection of Felix Klee, Bern, Switzerland. (K 73 Ib)*

48. Acrobats, 1919. Lithograph, c.195 × 77 mm. (compositon). *Collection of Professor Carl Djerassi, Stanford University. (K 71 IIb)*

49. Number-Tree Landscape, 1919. Lithograph, 175 × 126 mm. *Collection of The Robert Gore Rifkind Center for German Expressionistic Studies, Gift of the Robert Gore Rifkind Foundation, the Los Angeles County Museum of Arts. (K 72 IIb)*

50. Dying Light, 1919. Lithograph, 160 × 130 mm. *Collection of The Robert Gore Rifkind Center for German Expressionistic Studies, Gift of the Robert Gore Rifkind Foundation, the Los Angeles County Museum of Arts. (K 75b)*

51. Dying Light, 1919. Lithograph, c. 160 × 130 mm. (composition). *Collection of Professor Carl Djerassi, Stanford University. (K 75a)*

52. Three Heads, 1919. Lithograph, 126 × 148 mm. *Collection of The Robert Gore Rifkind Center for German Expressionistic Studies, Gift of the Robert Gore Rifkind Foundation, the Los Angeles County Museum of Arts. (K 70 IIIb)*

53. Three Heads, 1919. Lithograph, c. 125 × 150 mm. (composition). *Collection of Professor Carl Djerassi, Stanford University. (K 70 Ib)*

54. Insects (24th Plan of Creation), 1919. Lithograph with watercolor added using stencils, c. 205 × 148 mm. (composition). *Collection of Professor Carl Djerassi, Stanford University. (K 74)*

55. The Horrible Dream, 1919. Lithograph, c. 200 × 135 mm. (composition). *Collection of Professor Carl Djerassi, Stanford University. (K 76 IIb)*

56. A Genius Serves a Little Breakfast, 1920. Lithograph with water color, c. 255 × 175 mm. (composition). *Collection of Professor Carl Djerassi, Stanford University. (K 79 IIc)*

57. A Genius Serves a Little Breakfast, 1920. Lithograph without color, c. 255 × 175 mm. (composition). *Collection of Oeffentliche Kunstammlung Basel, Kupferstichkabinett. (K 79 I)*

58. Giant Aphid, 1920. Lithograph, 139 × 60 mm. *Collection of The Robert Gore Rifkind Center for German Expressionistic Studies, Gift of the Robert Gore Rifkind Foundation, the Los Angeles County Museum of Arts. (K 77 IIb)*

59. Hoffmannesque Scene, 1921. Color lithograph with three stones in black, yellow, purple c. 315 × 230 mm. (composition). *Collection of Kunstmuseum, Bern, Switzerland. (K 82IIc)*

60. Hoffmannesque Scene, 1921, Colored lithograph, 316 × 230 mm. (plate). *Collection of Kunstmuseum, Bern, Switzerland. (K 82I)*

61. Queen of Hearts, 1921. Lithograph, c. 255 × 175 mm. (composition). *Collection of Professor Carl Djerassi, Stanford University. (K 80b)*

62. The Saint of the Inner Light, 1921. Color lithograph with three stones, in black and two shades of tan, c. 310 × 175 mm. (composition). *Collection of Professor Carl Djerassi, Stanford University . (K 81IIc)*

63. The Loftier Aspect-Bauhaus Postcard, 1922. Hand colored lithograph, 144 × 73 mm. *Collection of Felix Klee, Bern, Switzerland. (K 88 Ib)*

64. Steamer for Lugano, 1922. Lithograph, c. 278 × 388 mm. (composition). *Collection of Professor Carl Djerassi, Stanford University. (K 83 IIb)*

65. Steamer for Lugano, 1922. Lithograph, 278 × 388 mm. *Collection of The Museum of Modern Art, New York, Purchase Fund. (K 83I)*

66. Buffoonery, 1922. Lithograph, c. 195 × 165 mm. (composition). *Collection of Professor Carl Djerassi, Stanford University. (K 84)*

67. The Witch with the Comb, 1922. Lithograph, c. 310 × 210 mm. (composition) *Collection of Professor Carl Djerassi, Stanford University. (K 86 Bb)*

68. Bauhaus Lantern Festival, 1922. Lithograph with watercolor. c. 90 × 145 mm. (composition). *Collection of Professor Carl Djerassi, Stanford University. (K 87b)*

69. Sun on the Gateway, 1923. Lithograph, 195 × 240 mm. *Collection of Kunstmuseum, Bern, Switzerland. (K 90)*

70. Striding Figure, 1923. Hand colored lithograph, 258 × 157 m.. *Collection of Felix Klee, Bern, Switzerland. (K 91)*

71. Collapsing, 1923. Hand colored lithograph, 191 × 274 mm. *Collection of Felix Klee, Bern, Switzerland. (K 93)*

72. Faces, 1923. Lithograph, 97 × 90 mm. *Collection of Felix Klee, Bern, Switzerland. (K 96)*

73. Tightrope Walker, 1923. Color lithograph with two stones, black and pink, 440 × 279 mm. *Collection of Felix Klee, Bern, Switzerland. (K 95)*

74. The Lighter Aspect-Bauhaus Postcard, 1923. Color lithograph with three stones, black, red, yellow, 104 × 145 mm. *Collection of The Art Institute of Chicago. (K 89 IVb)*

75. The Loftier Aspect-Bauhaus Postcard. 1923. Color lithograph, c. 140 × 75 mm. (composition). *Collection of Professor Carl Djerassi, Stanford University. (K 88 IIIb)*

76. The Man in Love, 1923. Color lithograph with two stones, black and tan , 275 × 190 mm. (composition). *Collection of Professor Carl Djerassi, Stanford University. (K 94 IIIb)*

77. The Singer of the Comic Opera, 1925. Lithograph with watercolor spatters, 412 × 283 mm. *Collection of Kunstmuseum, Bern, Switzerland. (K 99a)*

78. Ass, 1925. Lithograph, c. 240 × 160 mm. (composition). *Collection of Professor Carl Djerassi, Stanford University. (K 97b)*

79. Bearded Man, 1925. Hand water colored lithograph, 220 × 150 mm. *Collection of James Gilvarry, New York. (K 98Ac)*

80. Bearded Man, 1925. Lithograph, c. 220 × 150 mm. (composition). *Collection of Professor Carl Djerassi, Stanford University. (K 98Bb)*

81. The Heights, 1928. Etching, 230 × 230 mm. *Collection of Oeffentliche Kurstammlung Basel Kupferstichkabinett. (K 100)*

82. Girl's Head, 1928. Etching, 216 × 153 mm. *Collection of Felix Klee, Bern, Switzerland. (K 101)*

83. Underbrush, 1928. Etching on zinc with plate tone, 145 × 100 mm. (plate). *Collection of Professor Carl Djerassi, Stanford University. (K 102b)*

84. Juggler in April, 1928. Etching on zinc, 187 × 192 mm. (plate). *Collection of Professor Carl Djerassi, Stanford University. (K 103b)*

85. Old Man Reckoning, 1929. Etching on copper, 299 × 239 mm. (plate). *Collection of Professor Carl Djerassi, Stanford University. (K 104a)*

86. Never Ending, 1930. Etching, 177 × 137 mm. *Collection of Professor Carl Djerassi, Stanford University. (K 106)*

87. L'Homme approximatif, 1931. Etching and drypoint on copper, 178 × 140 mm. (plate). *Collection of Professor Carl Djerassi, Stanford University. (K. 107a)*

88. Prickle, the Clown, 1931. Liftground etching with aquatint, 290 × 340 mm. (plate). *Collection of Professor Carl Djerassi, Stanford University. (K 108b)*

89. Why Does He Run?, 1932. Etching on zinc with plate tone, 238 × 300 mm. (plate). *Collection of Professor Carl Djerassi, Stanford University. (K 109d)*

90. Marianne, n.d., Colored lithograph, 205 × 128 mm. *Collection of Maureen M. Morgan, Ardsley, New York.*

DRAWINGS*

91. Limping Girl With an Apple, 1904. Pencil and ink, 214 × 172 mm. *Collection of Kunstmuseum, Bern, Switzerland. (1904.16)*

92. The Hero With the Wing, 1905. Pencil, 214 × 115 mm. *Collection of E.W. Kornfeld, Bern, Switzerland. (1905.7)* (Preparatory drawing for K 16)

93. Self-Portrait (Conceived as a woodcut), 1909. Pen, brush, & ink, 168 × 240 mm. *Collection of Felix Klee, Bern, Switzerland. (1909.39[B])*

94. Bern, The Industrial Part of the Matte, 1909. Pen, brush, and ink, 217 × 255 mm. *Collection of Kunstmuseum, Bern, Switzerland. (1909.50)* (Preparatory drawing for K 32)

95. Bern, The Matte With the Minster Rising Above, 1910. Pen and ink, 173 × *151 mm. Collection of Kunstmuseum, Bern, Switzerland. (1910.50)* (Variant to K 32)

**Oeuvre numbers are given in paranthesis after the date.*

96. Houses on the Paradeground, Oberwiesenfeld Near Munich, 1910. Pen, brush,and ink, 211 × 407 mm. *Collection of Kunstmuseum, Bern, Switzerland. (1910.123)* (Preparatory drawing for K 33)

97. Munich Railway Station II, 1911. Pen & ink, 91 × 196 mm. *Collection of Kunstmuseum, Bern, Switzerland. (1911.25[B])* (Preparatory drawing for K 37)

98. Beyond All Doubt, 1912. Ink on lithographic transfer paper, 200 × 135 mm. *Collection of Felix Klee, Bern, Switzerland. (K A-117)*

99. Flight to the Stars, 1912. Ink on lithographic transfer paper, 145 × 122 mm. *Collection of Felix Klee, Bern, Switzerland. (1912.143[A]) (KA 120)*

100. Fabulous Island, 1913. Pen and ink, 60 × 194 mm. *Collection of Kunstmuseum, Bern, Switzerland. (1913.189)*

101. Acrobats and Juggler, 1916. Pen and ink, 241 × 128 mm. *Collection of Kunstmuseum, Bern, Switzerland. (1916.66)* (Preparatory drawing for K 71)

102. Number-Trees, 1918. Pencil, 164 × 112 mm. *Collection of Kunstmuseum, Bern, Switzerland. (1918.198)* (Preparatory drawing for K 72)

103. Inscription, 1918. Pen & ink, 210 × 750 mm. *Collection of Felix Klee, Bern, Switzerland. (1918.207)* (Preparatory drawing for K 88)

104. The Saint of the Inner Light, 1921. Pencil, 293 × 221 mm. *Collection of E.W. Kornfeld, Bern, Switzerland. (1921.158)* (Preparatory drawing for K 81)

105. Buffoonery 1922. Pencil, 233 × 166 mm. *Collection of E.W. Kornfeld, Bern, Switzerland. (1922.191)* (Preparatory drawing for K 84)

106. Man in Love, 1922. Pencil, 213 × 160 mm. *Collection of Galerie Rosengart, Lucerne, Switzerland. (1922.201)* (Preparatory drawing for K 94)

107. **The Witch With the Comb,** 1922. Pencil, 288 × 210 mm. *Collection of Galerie Rosengart, Lucerne, Switzerland. (1922.83)* (Preparatory drawing for K 86)

108. **Eye and Ear,** 1929. Pen and ink, 226 × 300 mm. *Collection of Galerie Rosengart, Lucerne, Switzerland. (1929.306)* (Preparatory drawing for K 107)

WATERCOLORS

109. **Passage from G.** 1927. Oil transfer watercolor, 12½ × 9½ in. Collection of James Gilvarry, New York (1927.75)

PORTFOLIOS AND BOOKS

110. **Sema-Mappe,** 1912. contains Klee's *View Over a River,* Lithograph 1912, plate 8. (K 42 Bb) *Collection of The Robert Gore Rifkind Center for German Expressionistic Studies, Gift of the Robert Gore Rifkind Foundation, the Los Angeles County Museum of Arts.*

111. **Schweizer Gruppe/Moderner Bund,** 1913. Second Mappe with 5 original prints by Paul Klee, Hermann Huber, Oskar Lüthy (etchings); Wilhelm Gimmi, Walter Helbig (woodcuts). Edition circa 40. Contains Klee's *Garden of Passion,* 1913 (K 56c), 97 × 146 mm. *Collection of Hans Bolliger, Zurich, Switzerland.*

112. **Zeit Echo,** 1914. (Graphik Verlag Munchen). Contains Klee's *Battlefield, 1914,* Lithograph, *(K 62II) and Death for the Idea,* 1914, Lithograph, (K 63 IIa) *Collection of The Robert Gore Rifkind Center for German Expressionistic Studies, Gift of the Robert Gore Rifkind Foundation, the Los Angeles County Museum of Arts.*

113. **Munchner Blatter fur Dichtung und Graphik,** 1919. George Muller Verlag, 305 × 235 mm. Contains Klee's *Acrobats,* 1919, Lithograph (K 71 IIb), *Three Heads,* 1919, Lithograph (K 70IIIb), *Number-Tree Landscape,* 1919, Lithograph (K 72IIb), *Insects,* 1919, Hand-colored Lithograph (K 74), *Meditation,* 1919, Lithograph (K 73IIb), *The Terrifying Dream,* 1919, Lithograph (K 76 IIb). *Collection of The Robert Gore Rifkind Center for German Expressionistic Studies, Gift of the Robert Gore Rifkind Foundation, the Los Angeles County Museum of Arts.*

114. **Das Kestnerbuch,** 1919. (Heinrich Bohme Verlag), 289 × 230 mm. Contains Klee's *Dying Light,* 1919, Lithograph (K 75B). *Collection of The Robert Gore Rifkind Center for German Expressionistic Studies, Gift of the Robert Gore Rifkind Foundation, the Los Angeles County Museum of Arts.*

115. **Die Schaffended Mappe,** 1919. (Herausgeber Paul Westheim, Gustav Kiepenheuer Verlag Weimar. I Jahrang. Herausgegeben 1919). 10 prints by Paul Klee, Feininger, Heckel, Modersohn-Becker, Mueller, Pechstein (2), Rohlfs (2), Schmidt-Rottluff. Contains Klee's *Small-World,* 1914, Etching on zinc (K 61). *Collection of Oeffentliche Kurstammlung Basel, Kupferstichkabinett.*

116. Voltaire's **Candide** or **The Story of the Best of Possible Worlds,** 1920. (Munich; Kurt Wolff Verlag), 255 × 195 mm. Book contains 26 reproduced ink drawing illustrations. *Collection of Professor Carl Djerassi, Stanford University.*

117. Voltaire's **Candide** or **The Story of the Best of Possible Worlds,** 1920. (Munich Kurt Wolff Verlag), 255 × 195 mm. Book contains 26 reproduced ink drawing illustrations. *Collection of The Robert Gore Rifkind Center for German Expressionistic Studies, Gift of the Robert Gore Rifkind Foundation, the Los Angeles County Museum of Arts.*

118. Curt Corrinth's Potsdamer Platz or **The Nights of the New Messiah. Ecstatic Visions,** 1920. (Munich, Georg Muller Verlag), 215 × 243 mm. Book contains 10 reproduced ink drawing illustrations. *Collection of The Robert Gore Rifkind Center for German Expressionistic Studies, Gift of the Robert Gore Rifkind Foundation, the Los Angeles County Museum of Arts.*

119. Deutsche Graphiker der Gegenwart (Kurt Pfister, ed.) 1920. (Leipzig, Klinkhart & Beirmann). Contains Klee's *Giant Aphid,* 1920, Lithograph, (K 77iib). *Collection of The Robert Gore Rifkind Center for German Expressionistic Studies, Gift of the Robert Gore Rifkind Foundation, the Los Angeles County Museum of Arts.*

120. Bauhaus Mappe I (Neue Europäeche Graphik, Erste Mappe), 1921. Meister des Staatlichen Bauhauses en Weimar. Produced and distributed by the Staaliches Bauhaus in Weimar in 1921, in collaboration with Muller Publishers, Potsdam. Includes 14 prints by Feininger (2), Itten (2), Marcks (2), Muche (1), Schlemmer (2), Schreyer (2) and Klee's *Saint of the Inner Light,* 1921, Color Lithograph (K 81) and *Hoffmannesque Scene,* 1921, Color Lithograph (K 82). *Collection of the Busch-Reisinger Museum, Harvard University, Cambridge, Massachusetts.*

121. Paul Klee, Pedagogisches Skizzenbuch (Bauhaus Book II), 1925. Albert Langen Verlag, Munich: 1925. Illustrations by Paul Klee; Typography and cover design by L. Moholy-Nagy. *Collection of Dartmouth College Library, Hanover, New Hampshire.*

122. L'Homme approximatif, Tristan Tzara, 1931. (Paris, Editions Fourcade) Contains Klee's *L'Homme approximatif,* 1931, Etching (K 107) *Collection of The Philadelphia Museum of Art.*

123. Laszlo Moholy-Nagy, *Untitled,* 1922. Watercolor, 554 × 690 mm. *Collection of Alice Adam Ltd., Chicago. Illinois.*

124. Laszlo Moholy-Nagy, *Untitled,* 1922. Woodcut, 573 × 662 mm. *Collection of Alice Adam Ltd., Chicago, Illinois.*

125. Vasily Kandinsky, *Small-World,* 1922. Color woodcut, 601 × 643 mm. (Cat. Roethel 168). *Collection of Alice Adam Ltd., Chicago, Illinois.*

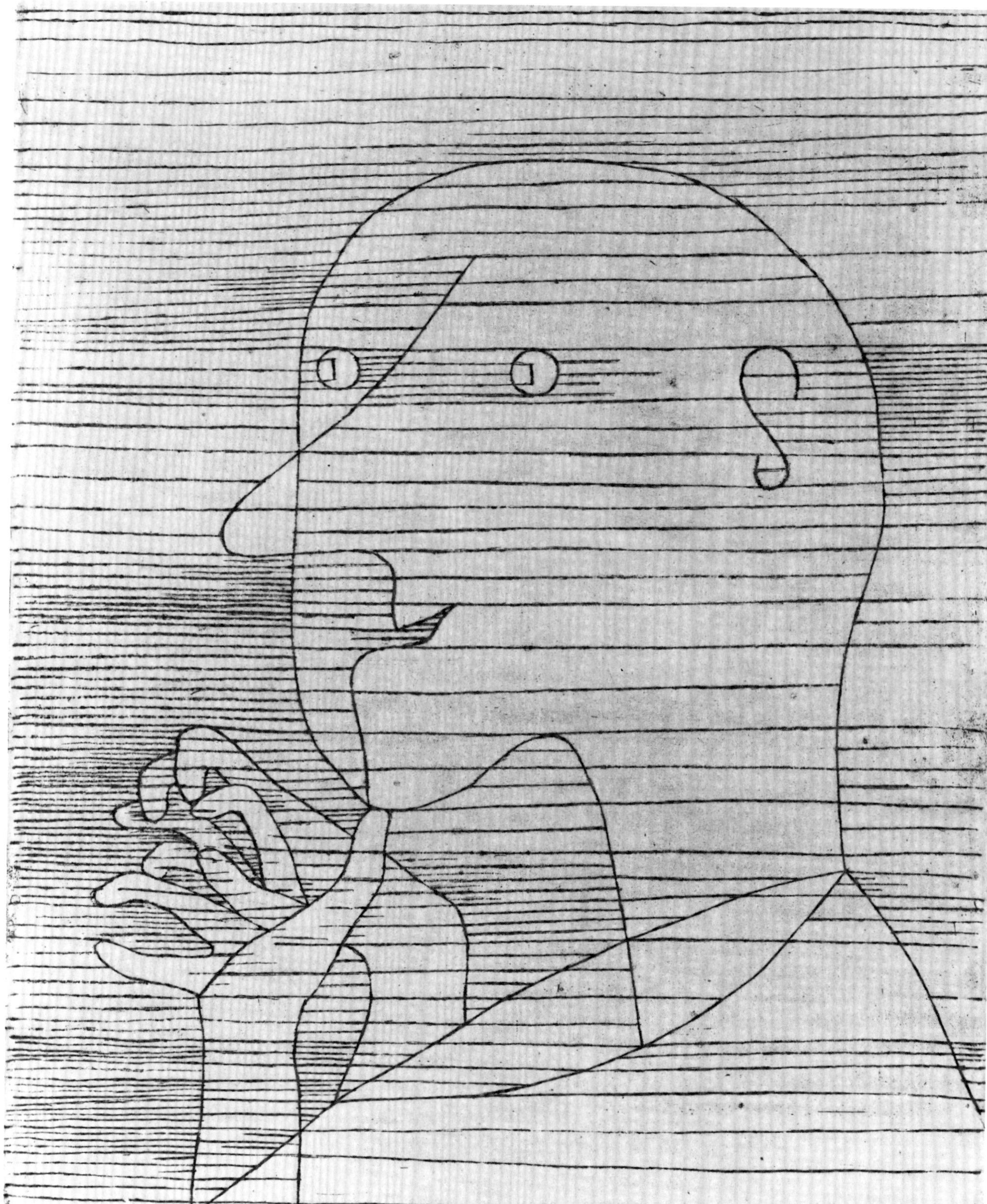

Old Man Reckoning, *1929. Etching on copper, 299 × 239 mm. (plate). Collection of Professor Carl Djerassi, Stanford University. (K 104a)*

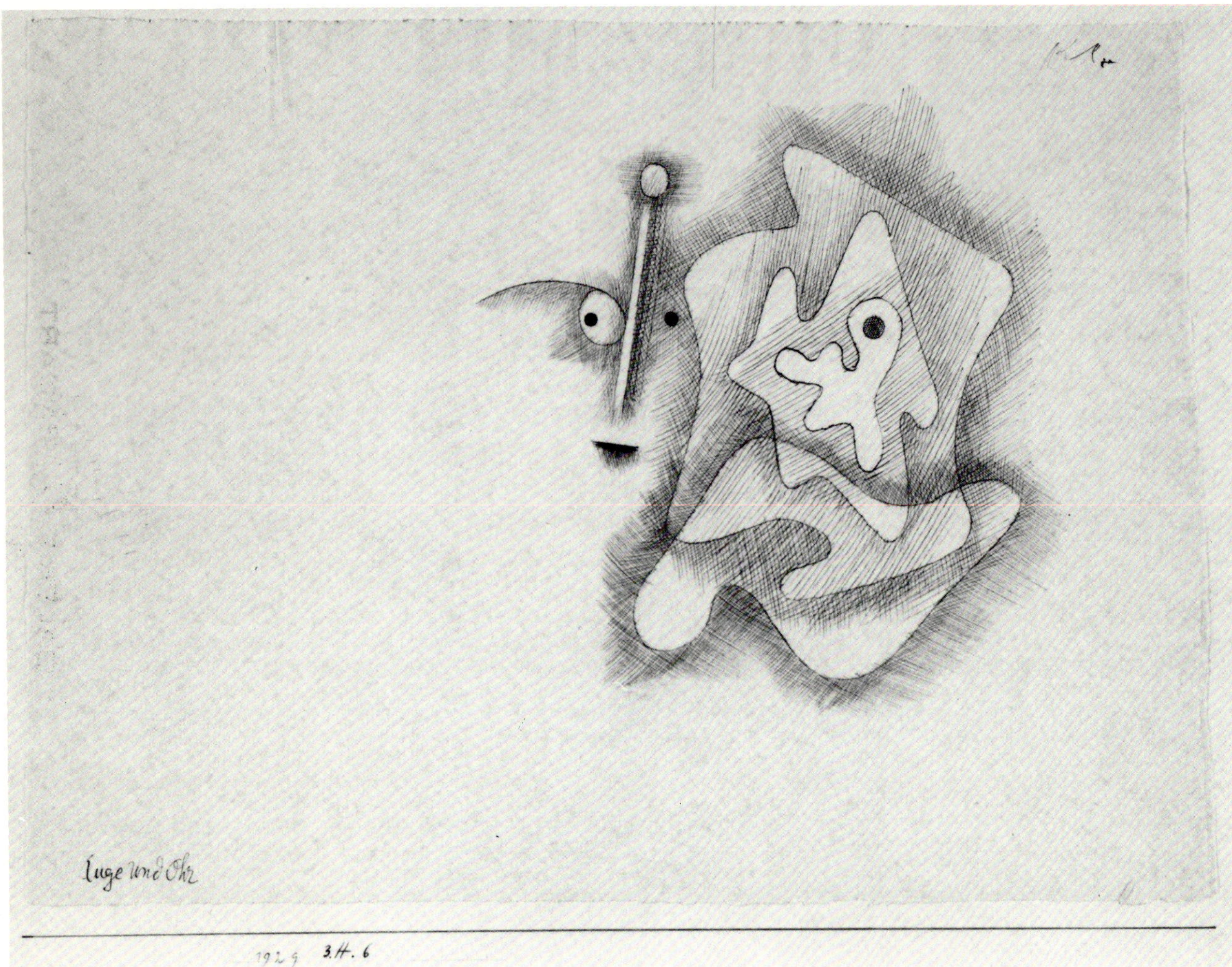

Eye and Ear, *1929. Pen and ink, 226 × 300 mm. Collection of Galerie Rosengart, Lucerne, Switzerland. (1929.306)*

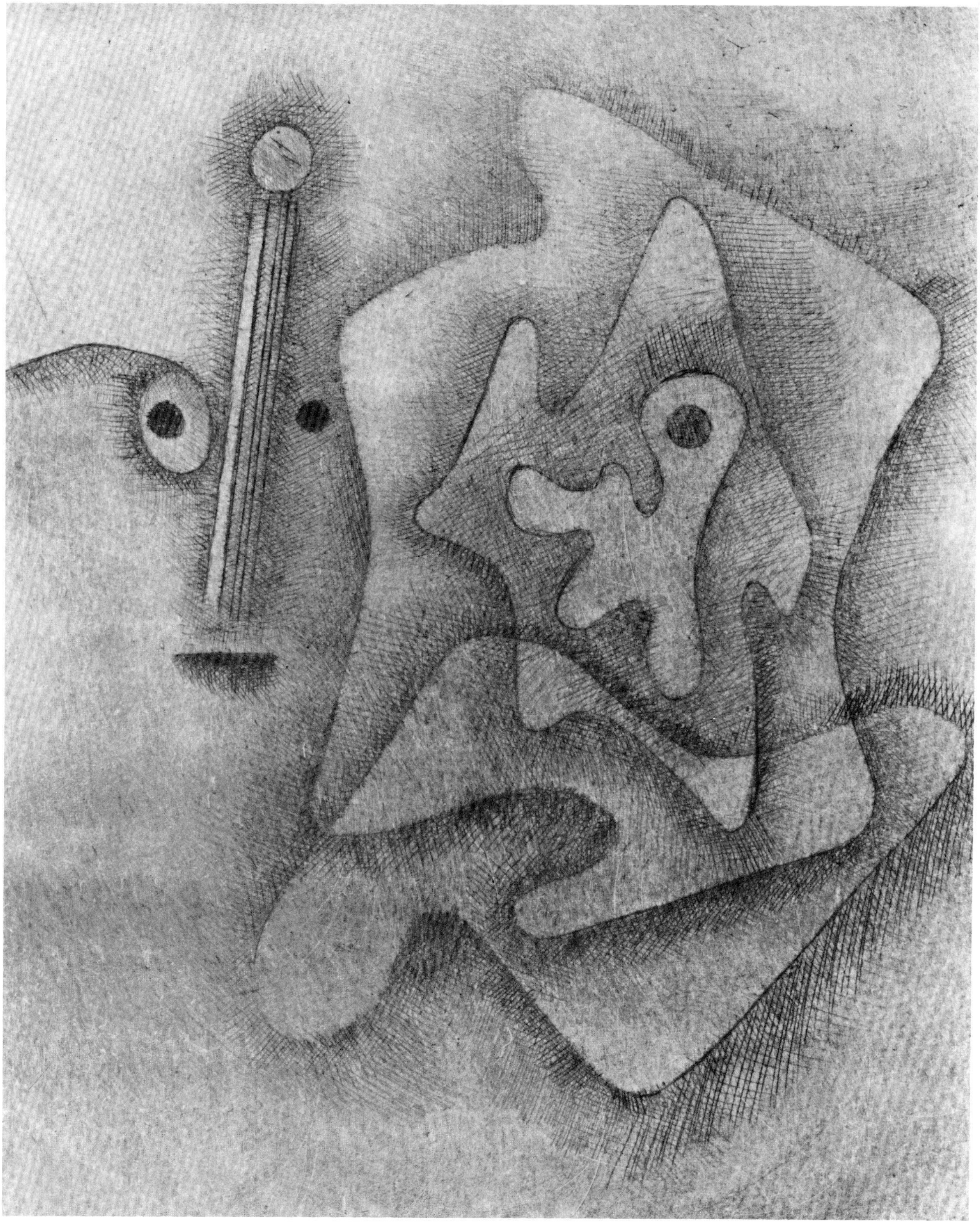

L'Homme approximatif, *1931. Etching and drypoint on copper, 178 × 140 mm. (plate). Collection of Professor Carl Djerassi, Stanford University. (K 107a)*

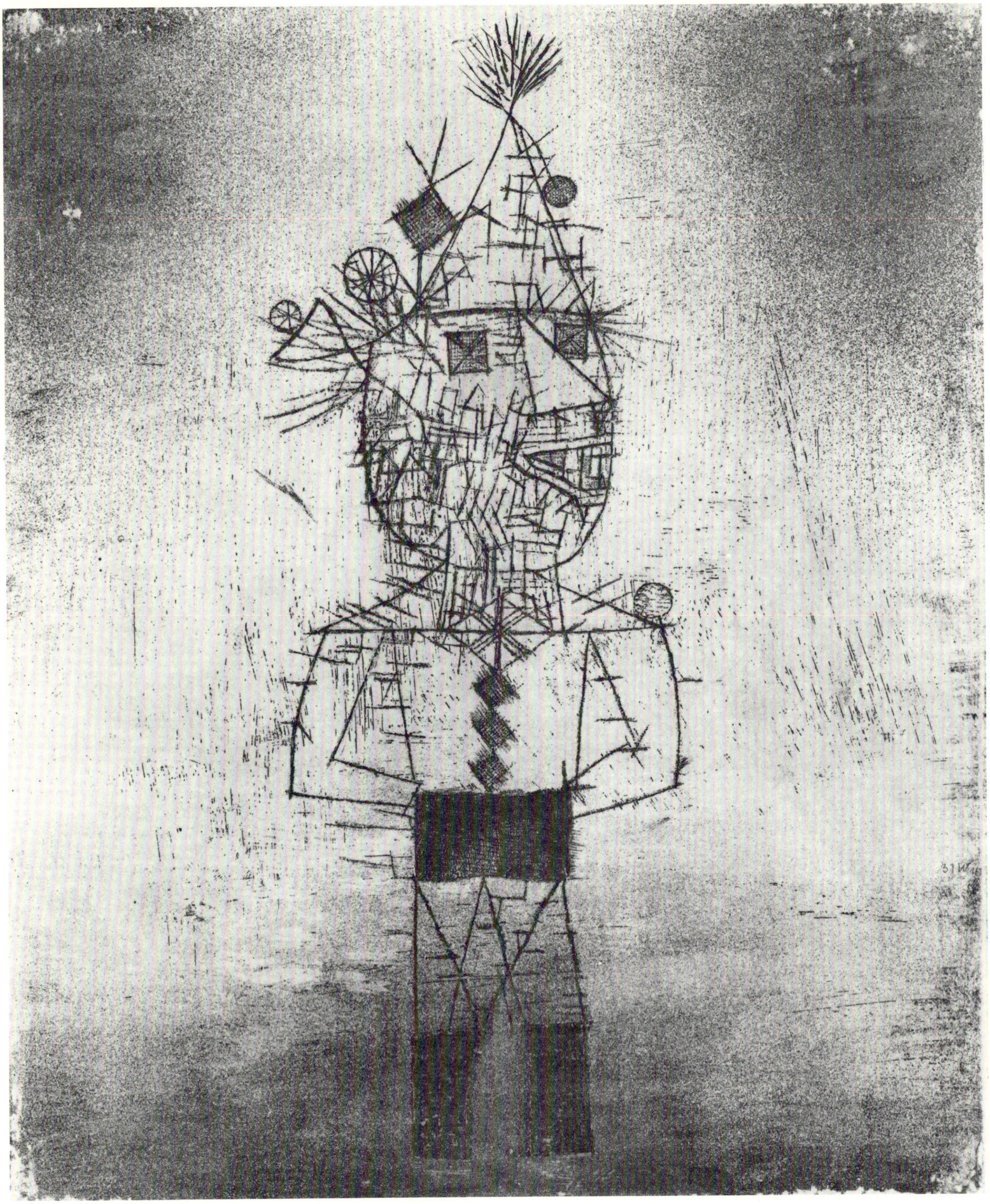

Prickle, the Clown, *1931. Liftground etching with acquatint, 290 × 340 mm. (plate). Collection of Professor Carl Djerassi, Stanford University. (K 108b)*

Why Does He Run? *1932. Etching on zinc with plate tone, 238 × 300 mm. (plate). Collection of Professor Carl Djerassi, Stanford University. (K 109 d)*